RIVER OF DOUBT

Martin Copeland

RAINBOW BRIDGE

Rainbow Bridge Books
2021

RIVER OF DOUBT

CONTENTS

FOREWORD   1

GLOSSARY OF SCREEN TERMS   3

PRINCIPAL CHARACTERS   5

ACT ONE   9

ACT TWO   63

ACT THREE 158

FOREWORD

In 1914 ex-US President Theodore Roosevelt, his
son Kermit and naturalist George K. Cherrie joined an expedition let by the already legendary
Brazilian explorer Col. Candido Rondon, his as-
sistant Lieutenant Lyra, physician Dr. Cjazeira
and their intrepid "camaradas" down a
completely unknown river in the heart of the
Amazon rainforest that Rondon had christened
the "River of Doubt."

This book is a fictionalization of that epic journey. It is written in screenplay form, for several
reasons but not least of them, a screenplay allows the personages to speak for themselves without the narrative voice to define and interpret.

Moreover, a film screenplay relies heavily on the
visual, and the reader is invited to imagine the
scenes depicted from a courageous journey
through a land whose primeval beauty astoun-
ded the explorers, even when a son watched over
a father who seemed to have only hours to live:

The scene is vivid before me. The black rushing river with
the great trees towering high above along the bank; the
sodden earth underfoot; for a few minutes the stars would
be shining, and then the sky would cloud over and the
rain would fall in torrents, shutting out sky and trees and
river.

NOTE: all illustrations are reproduced from photos by Kermit Roosevelt and others and included in *Through the Brazilian Wilderness*, Theodore Roosevelt's account of the expedition.

GLOSSARY OF SCREEN TERMS

EXTERIOR & INTERIOR -- indicates whether the scene occurs outdoors or in.

POV -- Point of view. What a character sees.

PAN -- camera movement. Can be as much as 360 degrees.

SERIES OF SHOTS -- simpler term for montage.

INTERCUT -- cinematic equivalent of counterpoint.

BEAT -- slight pause.

IN FRAME -- forefront of the scene.

V.O -- voice over the scene.

O.S -- off screen.

PRINCIPAL CHARACTERS

THEODORE ROOSEVELT -- former President of the United States, a locomotive of a man who shows no signs of slowing at 54. A stranger to doubt.

KERMIT ROOSEVELT -- Roosevelt's 24-year-old son, called "Bwana Dandy" for his elegant clothes and manner.

GEORGE K. CHERRIE -- a New England naturalist. Never allows war, rebellion and other distractions to impede his search for rare species.

COLONEL CANDIDO RONDON -- Brazil's greatest explorer. Descends the River of Doubt having never failed on an expedition. That record will be tested.

LIEUTENANT JOAO LYRA -- fiery and impulsive, fiercely loyal to Rondon for saving him from a life of miserable poverty, fiercely opposed to the Roosevelts.

DR. CAJAZEIRA -- Brazilian physician. Knows that in the Amazon, dangers may await beyond any man's imagining.

THE CAMARADAS -- loyal soldiers of Brazil.

ALICE LEE ROOSEVELT - Roosevelt's radiantly beautiful first wife. Dead for thirty years and banished from his memory.

In the wilderness a man reveals himself as he truly is.

--Theodore Roosevelt

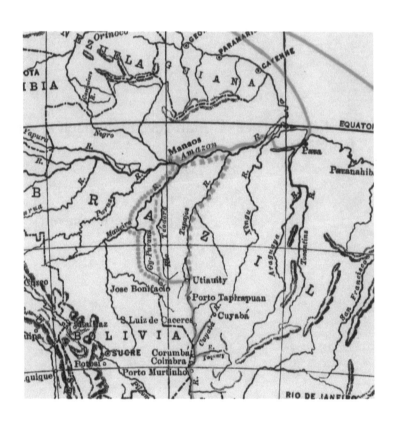

ACT ONE

EXT. OYSTER BAY, NEW YORK (EARLY 1890S) - DAY

A brooding spring twilight on the bay. Past banks bursting with foliage newly green--maple, oak, wildflowers and bloodroot--a JOHNBOAT is being rowed toward a neck of land.

THEODORE ROOSEVELT is at the oars and his thin, sickly 10-year-old son KERMIT sits in front. They are SINGING A BALLAD. Roosevelt, a man of seemingly limitless ebullience and energy, is in his early thirties at this epoch and leads the song lustily as is his style, filling in the words when youthful memory fails.

ROOSEVELT AND KERMIT
     (singing)
I do not like my billy goat,
I wish that he was dead,
Because he kicked me, so he did,
He kicked me with his head!

Roosevelt roars with his infectious laughter.

EXT. LANDSPIT - OYSTER BAY WOODS - DAY

Roosevelt is unloading blankets and food from the boat when he looks up to see Kermit coming out of the woods so burdened down with firewood he can hardly walk.

ROOSEVLT
Bravo, Kermit! Tonight we'll roast a gamebird.

TIME CUT

EXT. IN THE WOODS NEARBY - DAY

A REEDBIRD is chirping away, smugly perched,
uncognizant of its formidable foe

KERMIT

cached in the greenery close by, all ears as his
father lovingly cradles
A RUSTED 12-BORE PIN-FIRE.

ROOSEVELT
(softly)
The first weapon I ever owned, given to me by
your grandfather. He called it old "rust-bore."

He pats it lovingly, then hands the pitted and
rust-scarred gun to Kermit.

KERMIT
But I've never hit anything, Father. Even Alice is
a better shot.

ROOSEVELT
(pointedly)
That's why you're here, and the other children
aren't.

KERMIT
Yes sir.

ROOSEVELT
Now, what do I always say?

KERMIT
"Keep a cool head."

ROOSEVELT
Kermit, I've known many a crack shot who lost
his aim in the wild.

KERMIT
Yes sir.

Kermit puts the gun to his shoulder with some
difficulty.

ROOSEVELT
Got a tiny kick to it.

Roosevelt helps Kermit by propping the barrel
on a limb, then helping him sight. Roosevelt has
to squint through his pair of thick glasses.

ROOSEVELT
Tonight we roast a gamebird.

Kermit peers through the rifle sight--

INTERCUT

OLD "RUST-BORE" explodes in smoke and
flame--

THE REEDBIRD flies away SCREECHING.

THE TREETOP bursts with shattered leaves and
branches--

And OLD "RUST-BORE" is grabbed in mid-air by
Roosevelt, but he's not quick enough to catch
his son who falls ass-backwards from the gun's
kick, lands heavily in the mud.

Roosevelt shakes his head at his son's misad-
venture.

ROOSEVELT
Son, you can't roast a tree.

EXT. CAMPFIRE - NIGHT

Kermit sits around a vigorously burning campfire listening to his father spin a ghost story. He
is massaging his sore shoulder and trembling a
little.

ROOSEVELT
The wind whistled through the ancient castle
like a banshee. Whoo, whooo! So cold, Carothers
shook to the marrow of his spine; but after all, it
was only the wind. Wasn't it?
 Roosevelt eyes his son with some concern.

KERMIT
I'm not scared, father. It's the fever again.

Roosevelt nods, continues.

ROOSEVELT
If there were a poltergeist in the castle, he knew
he'd hear the telltale beating of a ghostly heart.
Whoo! went the wind. Whooo! CLANK ! What
was that!!?

BONK! BONK! Roosevelt bangs his fist against
the log on which he's sitting--

Kermit starts and YELLS, grabs Roosevelt's
shirt.

Roosevelt puts his arm around Kermit, pulls
him close to his side.

ROOSEVELT
Carothers felt an unmistakable surge of fear. He
knew if he didn't master it, all was lost. CLANK!
What was that?

Now Kermit has no fear. He nestles safe and
sure against his father as the ghost story continues.

EXT. OYSTER BAY - DAY (MORNING)

Mists rise on the river as the boat wends its way
back home. As Roosevelt rows, he HUMS a song.
The sound floats across the tranquil dawn water.

Kermit lies sleeping with his head on his father's lap.

OPENING TITLES ROLL OVER

A MONTAGE OF THEODORE ROOSEVELT'S CAREER

--Series of PHOTOS of Roosevelt and his Rough Riders. NEWSPAPER HEADLINES extol the heroic charge up San Juan Hill.

--NEWSREELS chronicle the homecoming of "the most famous man in America."

--INTERCUT NEWSREELS AND NEWS CLIPS:

--Roosevelt's election as governor of New York.

--As Vice President of the United States.

--McKinley's assassination.

--Roosevelt takes oath as president.

--He describes himself "strong as a Bull Moose." Later frequent references to his Bull Moose party.

--Reference to "gunboat diplomacy."

--Roosevelt declares his policy: "Speak softly and carry a Big Stick."

--Shots of laborers in Central American jungles slaving to construct the Panama Canal.

--Roosevelt's speeches, forceful bursts of pungent rhetoric eviscerating political opponents.

--Roosevelt's hunting expeditions.

--The "strenuous life."

--Roosevelt spares a bear cub and--

--The "Teddy Bear" is born.

--Roosevelt leaves office in 1908.

--His African safari. Roosevelt hunting. Among his kills: a water buffalo, eland, the lordly lion.

--Roosevelt at one of his happiest moments, kneeling behind the felled lion on the African veldt. At his side is a tall young man, incongruously dressed in white silk suit, smoking an expensive Meerschaum: KERMIT.

MONTAGE ENDS

SUPER TITLE: BRAZIL 1913

EXT. AMAZON JUNGLE - DAY

A group of BRAZILIAN EXPLORERS machete
their way up a hillock. BLADES swung by weary
arms slash at the thick tropical growth barring
their progress. SLASH! a thick frond falls, opening onto a SCREECHING MONKEY. Panicked,
it flees into the trees.

The men are so exhausted they hardly react.
Gaunt, bearded, almost naked, starved, they
breathe with difficulty. Some are too tired to
brush away the mosquitoes and boroshuda flies
gnawing on their arms and legs.

Two men are in the lead: COLONEL CANDIDO
RONDON, a leathery man who stands ramrod-
straight, and his younger LIEUTENANT JOAO
LYRA, fiery and impulsive.

THEIR POV

coursing through a jungle just as thick and
monstrous as they have just traversed is a river,
gleaming in the tropical sun.

LYRA
You know it?

Rondon shakes his head no.

MOMENTS LATER

Rondon takes measurements with a compass. He can hardly make the effort. He pants just from the sighting, squints from perspiration rilling his face. Lyra records the figures in a ledger so wet the pen scarcely makes impression.

RONDON
Latitude 12 degrees 1 minute south. Longitude 60 degrees, 15 minutes West.

VOICE (O.S.)
Coronel. Meu Coronel--

Rondon turns to the speaker, a MAN just now hobbling up to the group of exhausted men slumped on the ground waiting for Rondon and Lyra to finish. He is naked, famished. Every rib bone distends skin flayed red and raw by insect bites, falls, lashing vegetation.

Rondon stares at the man tottering before him on grave's edge, looks infuriated by his helplessness to aid.

LYRA (O.S.)
What shall we call this river?

RONDON
(a beat)
Duvida.

Rondon strides past the man. The others struggle to their feet, head into the jungle after him. Lyra is the last to follow. The man just stands there blinking, looking with death eyes--

HIS POV

the newly christened "RIVER OF DOUBT."

LEGEND: SOME MONTHS LATER

INT. PRESSROOM - AMERICAN MUSEUM OF
NATURAL HISTORY - DAY

ON ENLARGED MAP OF AMAZON JUNGLE

set on an enormous easel. It is painted green,
the Amazon River is printed in bold relief, but all
else is virtually blank. The emptiness is vast and
impressive.

ROOSEVELT (O.S.)
Gentlemen, when you consider the state of the
world's geography, I'm being given what very few
men will ever have again, the chance to explore
the complete Unknown.

Now we pick him up, pacing in front of the easel.
Theodore Roosevelt at 54 is brawnier, but still
possesses the same remarkable energy and
force.

ROOSEVELT
When I finish my South American speaking tour,
I'll rendezvous with the Brazilian exploring team.

THE GENTLEMEN OF THE PRESS

are taking notes. We remark in particular a bra-
shly curious YOUNG REPORTER.

Behind Roosevelt stand various museum offi-
cials and two men in particular: KERMIT ROO-
SEVELT and GEORGE K. CHERRIE.

Now in his early '20s, Kermit is lean, with an
elegance of manner, speech and taste. He wears
white pants, blue scarf and a silk shirt, all just
off the best racks at Abercrombie & Fitch.

Cherrie is in his '30s, a laconic New Englander
of the classic kind, capable of noting the exact
dimensions and species of a wild tiger even while
wrestling it.

YOUNG REPORTER
Colonel Roosevelt, where exactly is this unk-
nown river, the
    (checking his notes)
"Rio Duvida?"

ROOSEVELT
    (tapping the map)
Somewhere here. In the very heart of the Amazon jungle. No civilized man has ever been there.
Colonel Rondon is Brazil's greatest explorer,
knows the Amazon better than any man alive,
but until he discovered it last year no one had
the slightest idea it even existed. We're going to
put it on the map.

REPORTER #2
Sir, how does this compare to your African safari?

ROOSEVELT
Africa was a picnic. This is an adventure.

REPORTER #3
And the role of the museum?

ROOSEVELT
Mr. Cherrie--

CHERRIE
I've been asked to accompany Colonel Roosevelt
and gather specimens.

ROOSEVELT
Cherrie's a first-rate naturalist, made over 25
trips to South America. Says he's seen mosquitoes big as his thumb.
    (to Cherrie)
On San Juan Hill they ate thumbs for breakfast!

Laughter from all. Roosevelt points out Kermit.

ROOSEVELT
My son Kermit is going along to do what he did
so well in Africa, keep the old man capital company!

The reporters look to Kermit, notebooks poised.
Kermit shuffles awkwardly, finally forces out:

KERMIT
I'm looking forward to the trip.

No juicy quotes there. All eyes turn back to Roosevelt.

YOUNG REPORTER
Sir, during your presidency you astonished Americans with your adventures in the wilds, the so-called strenuous life. But if I may say so sir, you're almost 55 years old. Isn't this trip--

ROOSEVELT
(biting off the words)
Rugged? Exactly!
(big smile full of his famous teeth)
It's my last chance to be a boy.

INT. ROOSEVELT MANSION - DAY

Frantic family bustle of last minute packing and trip preparations, centered around Roosevelt who is a dervish of activity.

ROOSEVELT
Edith, my glasses!

EDITH ROOSEVELT
All packed.

She shows him 8 pairs of spectacles, all neatly arranged in a carrying case.

EDITH ROOSEVELT is an elegant woman in her fifties, still beautiful, accustomed to regulating her enthusiastic husband.

EDITH ROOSEVELT
Your clothes, too.

ROOSEVELT
Then by George I suppose I can rest easy.

EDITH ROOSEVELT
Theodore, you've never rested a day in your life.

TED, JR., a bold vigorous youth in his father's image, watches. He is wearing an army uniform. Roosevelt's daughter ALICE is there too, a lovely young woman almost 30.

ALICE
We're going to miss you terribly, Father.

ROOSEVELT
And I you, Alice. All of you.

TED
I still don't see why I can't come. I'm healthy and I can shoot rings around Kermit.

ALICE
You say.

ROOSEVELT
Ted, our country needs you here.

He angrily flings a pair of pants into a suitcase.

ROOSEVELT
Blast this see-no-evil President. Europe's going
to explode while we--

EDITH ROOSEVELT
Theodore!
(handing him two books)
Marcus Aurelius. The Stoic.

Roosevelt gets the hint, shuts up.

EXT. LAWN - SAGAMORE HILL - DAY

In b.g. the mansion, a lovely edifice gracing the
hilltop overlooking the bay. Kermit strolls with
BELLE WILLARD, his beautiful fiancee.

BELLE
How long will you be gone?

KERMIT
Hard to say. Six months?

BELLE
So long. He's always dragging you along on these
wild expeditions, trying to make you into his
image. Just because your father's the Bull
Moose doesn't mean you have to be.

KERMIT
He didn't want me to postpone the wedding. Said
we should go ahead. I refused.

He takes her in his arms.

KERMIT
What's a few months to a lifetime? It'll be spring in Madrid. They say the scent of blossoms is so strong you can hardly breathe. It'll be a great day, our wedding. I want my father there.

BELLE
I'm sorry to be so selfish.

She kisses him fervently.

INT. OFFICE - BRAZILIAN TELEGRAPH COM-MISSION - DAY

IN FRAME, Lyra--now clean, well-dressed, with that lean and tough look of peak physical fitness that comes after weathering rigorous expeditions. He paces angrily.

LYRA
It's insane! Insane!

He stalks out of FRAME, leaving in view his interlocutor, Rondon, elegant in a new suit.

RONDON
If we want to make the trip, we have to accept the conditions.

LYRA
Them.

RONDON
Yes.

Lyra looks skyward as if for succor from God,
but finds none, shakes his head.

RONDON
He's no ordinary man. In Africa-

LYRA
Different jungle. Different continent.

RONDON
He built the Panama Canal.

LYRA
Did he notice how many men died doing it?

He paces angrily.

LYRA
And his son? Some privileged rich boy who
thinks he's out to pot a few quail. I'll bet you
anything he wears silk suits, smokes a pipe and
reads poetry for fun.

RONDON
I don't like it. But we have no choice.

LYRA
The wildest part of the Amazon. Some didn't
make it back last time, remember?
(Rondon looks grim)
Does the dead man still call you?

Rondon doesn't reply.

EXT. HARBOR - RIO DE JANEIRO - DAY

A liner enters the harbor...

SUPER: DECEMBER 1913

EXT. PARAGUAY RIVER - DAY

A GUNBOAT YACHT steams up the tropical river.

INT. MAIN CABIN - DAY

Roosevelt is hunched over a desk, writing.

ROOSEVELT (V.O.)
In a strange land a man who cares for wild birds
and wild beasts always sees and hears something that is new to him and interests him.

SERIES OF SHOTS - RIVERBANK JUNGLE

picturing Roosevelt's descriptions.

ROOSEVELT (O.S.)
On the mud-flats and sand bars and among the
green rushes were stately water-fowl. Capybaras
sometimes stared stupidly at us.

SHOT

of a capybara, a sort of aquatic guinea pig as big
as a small sheep.

ROOSEVELT (V.O.)
Once we saw a herd of the fierce, white-lipped
giant peccary.

SHOT. They scurry into the jungle. As they disappear, POV FROM BOAT--we hear a curious
MOANING sound in their wake--plangent, ominous.

ROOSEVELT (V.O.)
Caymans were common.

SHOT. A cayman, its huge jaws opening wide,
frightening--a RIFLE SHOT rings out. The cayman flops over, dead, leaving IN FRAME the
passing gunboat, Kermit on deck lowering his
rifle.

The gunboat yacht steams around a wide turn.

EXT. DECK - GUNBOAT YACHT - DAY

Cherrie has joined Kermit at the railing.

CHERRIE
You really think I should tell him?

KERMIT
Absolutely.

CHERRIE
He won't like it.

KERMIT
If I've heard him say it once, I've heard it a thousand times. "The only thing worse than lying is a
skulker hiding the truth." I'd hate to see you
skulk, Cherrie.

Cherrie nods, turns away. Dubious but determined. Kermit cracks a smile at Cherrie's discomfi-
ture.

INT. ROOSEVELT'S CABIN - DAY

Cherrie enters tentatively. Roosevelt is writing
briskly, doesn't look up.

ROOSEVELT
Well, what is it, Mr. Cherrie?

CHERRIE
Col. Roosevelt, I think you should know a little
bit about me before we start this journey into
the wilderness.

Roosevelt goes on writing.

CHERRIE
I think you should know that I occasionally drink.

Roosevelt doesn't respond for a long moment. Cherrie is surprised. Then suddenly Roosevelt whirls around, looks him straight in the eye.

ROOSEVELT
Cherrie, you say you drink?

CHERRIE
Yes, I occasionally take a drink.

ROOSEVELT
What do you drink?

CHERRIE
Well Colonel, that depends a good deal on what is available.

ROOSEVELT
How much do you drink?

CHERRIE
All that I want.

ROOSEVELT
(shaking a finger at him)
Cherrie, just keep right on drinking!

He turns back to scrawling furiously. Cherrie gathers the interview is at an end.

ANGLE ON DRAFT RIVER STEAMER

cruising upstream for a rendezvous with Roosevelt's boat. On deck are Rondon and Lyra.

LATER - THE TWO BOATS

maneuver to a stretch of sand/mud beach with a spectacular view of the forest.

EXT. DECK OF RIVER STEAMER - DAY

Roosevelt steps aboard, followed by Kermit, Cherrie and the other members of his team. BRAZILIAN AND AMERICAN FLAGS are unfurled up respective masts. A small band launches into the U.S. national anthem. Roosevelt puts hand over heart. PAN THE REST OF HIS COMPANIONS: besides Kermit and Cherrie, FATHER ZAHM, FIALA, SIGG and LEO MILLER.

LATER

the Brazilian national anthem. Standing in resplendent white uniforms are the Brazilian contingent: besides Rondon and Lyra and a distinguished looking man, LAURO MULLER, there is DR. CAJAZEIRA, an efficient and practical physician. Behind them stands a group of mixed-blood men, tough, strong and sinewy: the CAMARADAS. Among them: SIMPLICIO, JULIO, PAISHON, PEDRINHO and ANTONIO.

LATER

Lauro Muller addressing the assembled groups:

MULLER
As Minister of Foreign Affairs, I often had the
wearisome duty to--what was the word you
used?

ROOSEVELT
"Slog."

MULLER
Slog through official meetings with presidents
and prime ministers. No meeting with Theodore
Roosevelt was ever that. Mr. President, Colonel,
it's a personal pleasure for me to confirm my government's backing to you and Col. Rondon in
this important work of exploration.

APPLAUSE. When it dies down--

ROOSEVELT
I've punched cows and gunslingers in North Dakota, dodged Mauser bullets on San Juan Hill,
hunted the lordly lion, and on my honeymoon,
slogged up the Matterhorn. But I've got a feeling
this trip will top them all. My dear sir, I thank
you from my heart.

He shakes Muller's hand to MORE APPLAUSE.
Both parties come together for handshaking, ac-
quaintance, small talk.

THE RECEPTION - SERIES OF SHOTS

A table set up on deck underneath an awning proffers much food and champagne, a real feast. In b.g. the camaradas bathe and swim in the river at beachside. Rondon and Roosevelt are looking over a large scale map laid out on a bulwark.

RONDON
In my 18 years exploring this area for the Telegraph Commission I've come to expect surprises, but when Lyra and I came upon a river this big, well, perhaps it drains into the Madeira, perhaps the Gy-Parana, perhaps it's an affluent of the Aripuana. I don't know. So I called it the "Duvida."

ROOSEVELT
A splendid name!

RONDON
It flows through a savage hell. The camaradas who came with us last time refused to go back. Perhaps they are wise.

ROOSEVELT
Colonel, thank you for that graceful way of saying it's not too late to back out. But like the Indians say, "Not for a hundred buffalo!"

BELOW DECK

Cherrie is showing Sigg, another naturalist, the collection of specimens he has amassed. Impressive: birds, small mammals, and a striking JAGUAR. Cherrie pats its flank.

CHERRIE
This one's thanks to Col. Roosevelt. The rest, yours truly.

SIGG
Amazing collection. And every one gathered on your trek here?

CHERRIE
Before breakfast and after dinner. I've never seen such variety and proliferation.

He arranges one of the bird specimens.

CHERRIE
I'll name this one after you. How about,"the grosbeaked Sigg?" Got a ring to it, don't you think?

Sigg doesn't look so sure.

ON DECK - SERIES OF SHOTS

picking up various conversations, first Roosevelt and Rondon, strolling--

ROOSEVELT
Kermit's Episcopalian, Father Zahm and Miller
Catholics, Sigg Lutheran, Cherrie Presbyterian. I
belong to the Dutch Reformed Church. And you,
Colonel?

RONDON
Positivist.

ROOSEVELT
Ah. In lieu of a religion, you have a philosophy.

RONDON
Yes. My only commandments are to treat my fellow man fairly, to live my life bravely, and no
less bravely face death.

DR. CAJAZEIRA

is showing Father Zahm and Fiala his medical
supplies and equipment.

DR. CAJAZEIRA
This ointment is particularly effective against the
boroshuda fly. Without it, why, I've seen the
blisters drive men to suicide. Two liters of quinine for the fever, antivenin for the jacares. I
don't expect to find that snake here, but in the
Amazon I prepare for everything I could ever
imagine.

FATHER ZAHM
And what of that you can't?

DR. CAJAZEIRA
I pray to the good God.

Cherrie is now at the drinks table, but before he can get a refill Roosevelt is at his side, pours his bubbly into Cherrie's glass.

ROOSEVELT
Everywhere I went on my tour, Chile, Bolivia-- champagne--Cherrie, I loathe the stuff.

Lyra watches from the deck as the camaradas cavort in the water.

LYRA
  (to the camaradas)
Eyes open!

Rondon is at the deck, too, watching the cama- radas. Roosevelt comes up. Rondon notes his empty glass.

RONDON
Très bon, le champagne.

ROOSEVELT
Merveilleux. J'en bu assez.

RONDON
If I speak French, it's because my English not so great.

ROOSEVELT
It's ten times better than my French, which I
speak as if it had no gender or tense.

A WHOOP from one of the camaradas, a tall
muscular man, draws their attention.

RONDON
That is Paishon. He and Pedrinho
lead the camaradas. Good fellows. We will need
them.

ROOSEVELT
Lauro Muller says your treatment of the Indians
is a model of sympathy and understanding.

RONDON
Their blood is in me.

Cherrie is now leaning beside Kermit over the
deck rail. Cherrie hears a bird call from the forest.

CHERRIE
I'd collected 84 birds, each one unnamed and
unclassified, when the museum wired me they'd
run out of funds. Luckily there was a revolution
on. I picked up the necessary funding running
guns. When my generalissimo won the war I
named a new species of wood thrush after him.
The "longtailed Felipe."

Cherrie waits for Kermit's approval. Out of poli-
teness:

KERMIT
Got a ring to it.

CHERRIE
     (proudly)
Doesn't it.

FATHER ZAHM

is sitting under a canopy, wiping his brow.

FATHER ZAHM
Ach, Schweinerei!

Lauro Muller comes up to Rondon.

MULLER
  (eyeing the camaradas)
They are reliable?

RONDON
We will find out soon enough.

MULLER
(nodding toward Roosevelt)
He is a great friend of our country. The president
and I greatly hope all will go well.

RONDON
Give the president my gracious compliments.
Tell him, Rondon does not fail.

Kermit finishes off the bottle of champagne by refilling Cherrie's glass, but before he can get another, Lyra comes up to them.

LYRA
(to Kermit)
They tell me you want to ride in the first boat.

KERMIT
Yes. I've done a lot of surveying work.

LYRA
Measuring a lacrosse field isn't the same as a wild jungle river.

KERMIT
Dam construction. In eastern Brazil.

LYRA
The lead canoe scouts rapids and obstructions in the current; one fallen limb can overturn a dugout. Indians. If the first time you see a poisoned arrow it's in your heart, if the camaradas can't understand what you say--

KERMIT
I've picked up the language pretty well.

LYRA
Let's be grateful for that.

He moves away.

CHERRIE
Pleasant fellow.

Cherrie takes the empty bottle from Kermit's hand.

CHERRIE
Your whistle needs wetting.

As he moves away to get a refill Kermit leans back over the railing. He looks down at the river, reflecting.

The water below is a beautiful greenish-blue. Still, pellucid. The reflection of tropical leaves forms a lovely tableau, like a Monet garden.

Kermit plays with the reflection, holding the champagne glass over the water. Catching sun-beams, the reflected glass fairly sparkles in the water.

Kermit notices something. He looks closer.

HIS POV

the stillness of water is rippled by the swift pas-sage of a small fish. Then another. Another, swimming rapidly.

A SCREAM rends the festivities.

A WOUNDED CAMARADA

knee-deep in the water, is flailing helplessly.

The other camaradas are clambering frantically out of the water. Only Paishon has the grit to hustle over, grab his fellow camarada and muscle him onto the steamer's deck.

PIRANHA are clinging to the camarada's leg. Pedrinho takes an oar, tries to beat them off--only partially succeeds.

Dr. Cajazeira rushes up, begins to administer first aid as the wounded camarada, howling in pain, is laid down on deck.

All crowd around to see the sight: the camarada's right big toe has been bitten completely off. It shoots blood.

Now safely on deck himself, Paishon shouts what happened in Portuguese.

LYRA
Piranha.

KERMIT
(to Roosevelt)
Cannibal fish. He cut his foot on a stone. Blood drives them insane. They would have ripped every ounce of flesh from his bones.

Pedrinho lets drop the oar on deck, and we see why. PIRANHA are still clinging to it, their teeth inbedded in the wood. One buries its teeth, CRACK.

The others flap on deck, uttering a strange SQUEALING sound. One flops onto a cloth and seizes it with a bulldog grip.

A piranha attacks another, biting savagely into its body, SQUEALING with fury.

Roosevelt looks stunned by the ferocity he's witnessing.

The wounded camarada SCREAMS, writhes in pain.

LATER

swabbed in bandages, he is lifted on his palette onto the steamer. That done, the steamer begins to head away from the gunboat, which with a ROAR of its engines moves in the opposite direction toward its rendezvous.

Roosevelt and Rondon

EXT. RIVERBANK - DAY

All manner of equipment--cartons of food, medical supplies, rifles--is being readied for a pack
train of horses and mules tethered nearby. The
exploring party mill about inspecting provisions,
chatting. In b.g. the gunboat rests at anchor.

PAISHON

While supervising the camaradas who are doing
the bulk of the work loading provisions, he notices that one, Julio, is lounging around. He
barks a command in Portuguese and Julio re-
turns to work, not with alacrity.

RONDON

with his dog LOBO who will accompany him in
his boat down the river, is looking over the goods
with Fiala.

FIALA
I sent a pack train ahead with the first load of
supplies.
(Rondon nods approval)
What do you think of my preparations?

RONDON
I'm amazed. Col. Roosevelt said you had never
even seen the jungle.

ROOSEVELT
He lives in New York. Same difference.

He laughs. Roosevelt is in fine form. He moves
over near the gunboat, yells up at the COOK
who is watching the packing.

ROOSEVELT
Join the expedition, Mario! Always room for a
cook with your culinary genius.

COOK
Señor Roosevelt, I have done nothing to deserve
such punishment.

Roosevelt again roars with laughter.

Kermit is arranging his goods. He is dressed in
white, has a rakish hat.

Roosevelt stops by, notes a book in Kermit's duffel. Lyra does, too.

ROOSEVELT
Ah, after food and clothing, the most vital provi-
sion. I'm taking Greeks. You?

Kermit lights his pipe.

KERMIT
The Oxford Book of French Verse.

Lyra shakes his head. It's as he figured.

Roosevelt hands Kermit his rifle.

ROOSEVELT
Clean as a whistle, thanks to your meticulous
parent. If only you kept your firearms as clean
as your suits.

Kermit ties a purple scarf around his neck. Antonio and Simplicio have been standing nearby
watching him, muttering bemused admiration.

KERMIT
They like my outfit.

ROOSEVELT
     (to the 2 camaradas)
In Africa they called him "Bwana Merodati."
Bwana Dandy.

Antonio and Simplicio try to pronounce "Bwana
Dandee."

Lyra eyes the pipe-smoking poetry-reading
"Bwana Dandy" and just shakes his head as
Kermit begins to fold with great care a white suit
into his duffel.

LYRA
Silk?
     (Kermit nods)
I thought so.

He mounts his horse, casts an I-told-you-so
glance at Rondon, who climbs onto his mount as
well, looks down at Kermit who is not having
much success packing his extensive wardrobe.

RONDON
We will need almost a month to reach the Duvida. It will be a hard ride. Silk may not survive.

He turns, heads his horse away.

MOMENTS LATER

the caravan, an impressive sight, so many are
the horses and men, moves out.

Kermit Roosevelt

EXT. ON THE TRAIL - DAY

Roosevelt and Rondon ride beside each other.
They ride out of FRAME and we PAN DOWN to
the horses' hooves, moving through this grass-
land.

MATCH CUT - MANY DAYS LATER

hooves this time sloshing through mud, a thick
viscous swamp of it, the horses breathing hard,
wearily.

SUPER: FEBRUARY 1914

EXT. MUD BOG - DAY

Roosevelt, riding beside Rondon, turns in his
saddle, eyes the expedition. Men are weary, the
animals emaciated and scrawny from the long
haul.

ROOSEVELT
We're showing some bones.

RONDON
I thought it best to ration provisions for the river.

ROOSEVELT
And if we run short there?

RONDON
If worse comes to worst, we can live off fish and
Brazil nuts.

LYRA

rides up next to Kermit.

LYRA
Tomorrow we reach the land of the Parecis.
Some say they eat human flesh. If this makes
you nervous, stay with the camaradas.

KERMIT
My father always says, "no nerves, no courage."

The debate might continue, but suddenly a sight
makes them rein up.

SERIES OF SHOTS

of bones and skulls littering the ground, car-
casses of men and animals who have come this
far but no farther. Roosevelt stares intently at A
CRATE upended, broken, its contents spilled
and already fallen prey to scavengers. A stenciled label reads:
EXPEDICO SCIENTIFICA ROOSEVELT-RONDON

ROOSEVELT
The advance party?

RONDON
They were fine men.

ROOSEVELT
But not fine enough.

He spurs ahead.

EXT. JUNGLE HILL - DAY (SUNSET)

Roosevelt and Kermit scramble up through vine-
covered trees, reach a promontory, look out over
tropical forest to a rich gold and orange sunset
sky through broken rain clouds.

ROOSEVELT
We've seen a few skies, eh?

KERMIT
Remember the ones in Arizona and Sonora, at
sunset?

ROOSEVELT
Like red fire on a griddle.

KERMIT
North Dakota, when we hunted bear and cou-
gar?

ROOSEVELT
Autumn at Sagamore Hill. Gold and brown, like
the sky's draining color from the leaves.

KERMIT
Mount Kenya. The Guasa Nyiro.

ROOSEVELT
Ah, now that was something.

KERMIT
The best, for my money.

ROOSEVELT
They were all the best.

They smile, enjoy their memories for a silent
moment.

KERMIT
Rondon and Lyra doubt my fiber.

ROOSEVELT
They do, yes.

KERMIT
If I were Ted, Jr.--

ROOSEVELT
Don't tell me who you're not! Prove them wrong.

KERMIT
(getting the message)
Yes sir.

Roosevelt claps his son on the back for encouragement, turns back down the way they've come.
After a last look at the sky, Kermit follows.

EXT. PARECIS VILLAGE - DAY

The expedition trails into a clearing precariously
carved out of the primeval. The curious tribe exit

their huts en masse to greet the explorers, crowd around men and animals, shout and talk excitedly.

The Parecis, men and women alike, are virtually nude, but as the expedition's first arrivals begin to dismount among the crowd, we remark some men conspicuously clad in trousers and an occasional shirt with stenciled lettering.

KERMIT
(to Cherrie)
Easy to see who works for the Telegraph Commission.

Roosevelt is surrounded, center of attention of a throng.

ROOSEVELT
(to Dr. Cajazeira)
By George, they adore my spectacles!

DR. CAJAZEIRA
First ones they've ever seen.

One PARECIS YOUNG WOMAN seems particularly fascinated, reaching up tentatively to touch them.

ROOSEVELT
Blast, why not.

He gives the spectacles to the woman. She squeals excitedly, holds them like a precious object, runs off to hoard the prize, followed by a half-dozen curious friends.

EXT. PARECIS VILLAGE - DAY

Roosevelt and Kermit stroll in the middle of the village, observing with great interest the life around them. One woman weaves a cloth, another a hammock. Several children parade about on stilts.

Women are cooking melons and vegetables over open fires.

SERIES OF SHOTS

--Rondon is in conference with a group of Parecis. The chief, clad in the clothes signaling his labor for the Telegraph Commission, is among them, He gestures animatedly. Rondon nods.

--Julio is making crude advances toward a village woman who brushes off his arm, hurries away.

--Dr. Cajazeira is showing the Indian woman who received Roosevelt's spectacles how to put them on her nose.

ROOSEVELT
White men have brought so many horrors to native people. I'm afraid that's another.

A SHORT TIME LATER - CLOSE ON BALL

round or more correctly, mostly round, a rude
weave-and-stitch fabric wound over rubber
about eight inches in diameter, being dropped in
the dust.

PULLING BACK

a group of male Parecis CHARGE like soccer
players.
 The nearest to reach the ball dives into the dirt,
butts it WITH HIS HEAD. Another does the
same.

Roosevelt, Kermit and Cherrie are watching
along with the camaradas and many excited villagers. They watch for a moment.

CHERRIE
They call it "headball."

KERMIT
Original.

Kermit and Roosevelt have the same thought.
Turn to each other--

ROOSEVELT AND KERMIT
(chanting together)
I do not like my billy goat,
Because he kicked me, so he did,
He kicked me with his head!

They share a laugh.

THE PARECIS VILLAGERS

begin to crowd around the playing area, reacting and chattering like any sports crowd before a big game.

CHERRIE
They've challenged the camaradas to a game.

The respective players, Parecis and camaradas, are huddling, discussing strategy.

Rondon sits down next to Roosevelt, who is taking a keen interest in the upcoming game and all preparations for it.

Lyra comes up to Kermit and Cherrie with a flagon of wine and some large, gourd-shaped drinking vessels. He pours, offers one to Kermit.

LYRA
They make an excellent pineapple wine. Strong.

KERMIT
I never drink alone.

He stares, makes no move to accept Lyra's offer. Face-off.

CHERRIE
I do.

He takes the cup, drinks. Face-off ended, Lyra pours wine into the two remaining cups, keeps one for himself, gives the other to Kermit.

LYRA
Your health.

Kermit counters with a similar toast--in Portuguese.

RONDON
(to Roosevelt)
I asked them what sort of Indians we were likely to encounter. They cannot say. None of them has ever descended the River of Doubt.

ROOSEVELT
That's odd. It's in their backyard.

RONDON
Too much afraid.

Cherrie and Kermit are laughing over a joke and the wine when they suddenly realize Paishon and a TALL, FEARSOME PARECIS, captain of his team, are standing in front of them. In b.g. two opposing teams of headballers stare.
 Cherrie and Kermit have no trouble realizing what's being asked.

LYRA
I'll play!

He hops to his feet. Stares down at Kermit. Another challenge. Cherrie and Kermit search for excuses.

CHERRIE
It's not my sport, fellas. I'm an egghead.

He smiles at the joke. The Parecis captain doesn't. Cherrie tries again.

CHERRIE
(scratching his head)
Dandruff.

The Parecis captain glowers. Kermit nudges Cherrie:

KERMIT
You notice something funny about these cups?

Kermit stands. Cherrie takes the hint and notes they have a distinctive shape--like a man's skull.

KERMIT
Use it or lose it.

Cherrie jumps to his feet and--

A SHORT TIME LATER

hurtling into FRAME, landing on his face with a WHOOSH is Cherrie. He's missed the ball and eaten dirt. Roosevelt bellows a laugh.

Kermit gives Cherrie a hand up. Not daunted, they charge back into the fast and furious action. If enough players strike the ball well it remains in the air, being batted from head to head. If not and the ball hits the ground, headlong dives are necessary--and any sort of headbutt can occur in the melee.

SHOUTING, CHANTING, all the villagers crowd around, attracted by the competition between native sons and outsiders,. Among them we notice the young village woman wearing Roosevelt's spectacles; she is staggering like a drunk, unable to focus through the thick lenses.

Kermit and Cherrie are giving their all. Kermit runs, butts the ball in mid-flight to Simplicio who sends it over to Antonio (Roosevelt SHOUTS encouragement). Lyra plays fiercely, exchanges elbows
with Kermit.

FOLLOWING THE BALL

Heads pound the ground. Cherrie looks befudd-led, giving proof to his claim to be amateur. The ball goes repeatedly past his head, which butts only empty air.

ROOSEVELT
(to Rondon)
He's a good sport, Cherrie.

As if to prove the point Cherrie dives, misses the ball, collides heads with a Parecis. CRACK. Roosevelt and Rondon wince.

The action grows more intense, the crowd loud and shrill, the game hinges on the next shot--Kermit runs furiously, chasing the ball, charging in a crowd, elbowing aside Lyra and 2 Parecis (Roosevelt jumps to his feet), diving--his fore-head hits the ball flush, sending it flying in an arc over everybody's heads and ONTO THE TOP OF A HUT.

For a moment all stand in awe of this magnificent shot--then SHOUTS, CHANTING from the village women, all crowding around Kermit whose face is a mess of mud and dirt.

ROOSEVELT
Bully son, eh!

Roosevelt's teeth flash in a grin of exuberant pride. Lyra, tired and panting hard, doesn't show the same appreciation for Kermit's exploit.

EXT. PARECIS VILLAGE - DAY

The expedition ride out, waving goodbye to all the villagers gathered bidding farewell.

EXT. IN THE JUNGLE - DAY

riding through a torrential rain--

KERMIT

has his face upturned to the sky, welcoming the shower bath. He spits water.

KERMIT
My throat is one big mudpie.

LYRA
(riding past)
When I was a child, sometimes mud was all I had to eat.

Kermit doesn't reply, lets Lyra ride on past, but Cherrie, who's riding beside Kermit has a word:

CHERRIE
I'd name a bird after him, but in this part of the world there are no grouse.

LATER

WHACK! A camarada's machete slices vines and green tendrils, creating a path through green jungle wall. The expedition ride through under a persistent rain.

Rondon rides beside Roosevelt. As they splash through a swelling stream--

RONDON
Affluent of the Duvida.

Roosevelt casts an eager glance in passing as the rising stream swells anew from a burst of rainfall.

ANOTHER AREA OF JUNGLE

The rain over, STEAM MIST exhales from every leaf and tree, rises from the ground and the breath of the humans. WHACK! WHACK! WHACK! The machetes do their work.

POV LEAD RIDERS

Fronds, giant leaves and vines falling.

ROOSEVELT

impatiently spurs his horse forward beside Julio, reaches and grabs Julio's machete from its saddle scabbard.

ROOSEVELT
Tired already, Julio?

Without waiting for an answer, Roosevelt begins to hack his own way through the vegetation. Vigorous, bold stroking and cutting that carry him to the head of the group.

Thus he is the first to suddenly hew into a clearing--

He reins up. Kermit spurs up beside him.

THEIR POV

SEVEN DUGOUT CANOES are drawn up on a bank beside a wide streak of silver water that glistens in the searing sun, flows swathlike into the tropical forest.

KERMIT
The River of Doubt.

ACT TWO

EXT. RIVERBANK - DAY

PANNING THE DUGOUTS--two are dark with damp and moisture.

They seem barely able to hold water. Only half-filled with the expedition's provisions, they ride almost at water level.

A shoe KICKS one of the dugout canoes--Roosevelt's. He shakes his head at the condition of the boats.

ROOSEVELT
Floatable. Just.

RONDON
They were all Luiz could find.

ROOSEVELT
Not a trusty Maine birchbark, eh?

RONDON
We can lash the bad ones together and form a balsa.

ROOSEVELT
Bully idea.

Paishon comes up to Kermit.

PAISHON
You must choose your boatmen.

Kermit looks no further than Simplicio and Antonio, who are waiting for just such a nod. Smiles are exchanged.

LATER

Fiala, Sigg and the others are mounted, facing the Roosevelt-Rondon group who, with the exception of Roosevelt and Rondon, are already seated in the canoes.

RONDON
(addressing the riders)
You should have no trouble finding your depar-
ture point on the Papagaio. Descending from
there, then down the Tapajos, God willing you
will be waiting for us in Manaus. Colonel, do you
wish to say something?

ROOSEVELT
Only this. The ordinary traveler has no idea of
the risks and hardships faced by the first explorers. They walk on a trail blazed by very brave
men. Good luck, boys.

FIALA
The same to you, Colonel. The same to all of
you.

As Roosevelt and Rondon step into their respective boats, Rondon pauses a moment.

RONDON
I have a daily ritual called "the orders of the
day." Today they are, "Explore this river and
come back safely."

He sits down to hearty seconds and applause.

The boats push off into the River of Doubt.

ROOSEVELT
(to the riders)
We'll see you in Manaus!

FIALA
(softly)
God willing.

He turns his horse, leads the others riding back
into the jungle.

PANNING DOWN AND AWAY from them as the
last rider disappears into the jungle, we see the
boats of the Roosevelt-Rondon party already far
down the river.

CLOSER IN FRAME is one of the empty provi-
sion crates left behind. Rapacious FIRE ANTS
are already swarming over it.

EXT. ON THE RIVER OF DOUBT - ROOSE-
VELT'S CANOE - DAY

ROOSEVELT (V.O.)
On February 27, 1914, shortly after midday, we
started down the River of Doubt into the unknown.

SERIES OF SHOTS

MIRRORING Roosevelt's recorded impressions.

ROOSEVELT (V.O.)
It was delightful to drift and paddle slowly down the beautiful tropical river, down the swirling brown current through the vivid rain-drenched green. The lofty and matted forest rose like a green wall on either hand; there were not many birds; rarely we heard strange calls from the depths.

Just such a STRANGE CALL now echoes from the forest.

ROOSEVELT

looks up from his writing, toward the source of the sound.

HIS POV

the call ECHOES from within the jungle, but as the canoes drift away, nothing appears in sight.

Two camaradas, Julio being one of them, paddle this dugout. Cherrie accompanies Roosevelt.

Roosevelt notices Cherrie staring at him and his notebook.

ROOSEVELT
Articles for Scribner's, recording our adventures.

CHERRIE
A lot of extra work, that.

ROOSEVELT
I have to pay for my fun.

EXT. RIVERBANK - DAY

Kermit is squinting through a surveyor's sighting rod, signaling to Lyra upstream who esta-
blishes the distance with a telemeter.

Rondon in his canoe takes the direction with a
compass, makes a record of it.

Meanwhile Simplicio, in Kermit's canoe, is peering into the depths of the water.

DR. CAJAZEIRA
(to Roosevelt)
He looks for piranha. The camaradas have a su-
perstition. If even the devil fish avoid a river, it is
a river of death.

ROOSEVELT
Nonsense. All it means is we can take a swim!

Kermit gets back in his canoe, handing the rod
to Simplicio, who says something.

KERMIT
(translating)
He sees no fish.

BACK ON THE RIVER - CLOSE ON FALLEN
TREE

stretching almost across the river, narrower
here. The current whirlpools around the obs-
tacle.

IN THE BOATS

the backs and arms of the muscled camaradas
stretch with effort. Paddles dip, stroke on stroke.

Kermit in the lead canoe spots the obstruction,
barks an order. A flurry of hard paddling and the
canoe veers left, just avoiding the potentially
deadly branch.

Lyra and Kermit exchange a look as this first
test is successfully passed.

As Roosevelt floats by, he eyes carefully the fallen branch.

ROOSEVELT
A baritana palm. They love the wet.

EXT. RIVERBANK - DAY

the boats are anchored on a placid stretch.

EXT. STREAM BESIDE RIVER - DAY

The Americans are bathing in the rippling
stream. Kermit climbs out.Cherrie is already
drying off, or trying to. He sweats profusely.

CHERRIE
Hardly worth it to dry off.

Roosevelt lolls in the water, regards the forest all
around.

ROOSEVELT
(musing)
We need wilderness. That primeval fear our ancestors felt in the caves, it braces the soul.

LATER - AT THE RIVER

As Roosevelt, Kermit and Cherrie come up from
the stream.

Rondon is directing the camaradas to line up
behind him. That done, he stands at attention,
unrolls a sort of scroll from under his arm. Behind him Paishon and Simplicio are holding a
post they have carved from a small felled tree.

RONDON
(aloud to all)
Gentlemen, the orders of the day. As the official
representative of the Brazilian government, and
as this unknown river is evidently a great river, I
now formally christen it the "Rio Roosevelt."

The camaradas shout approval.

Roosevelt looks surprised.

ROOSEVELT
This comes as a total surprise. I'm touched but
the River of Doubt is an unusually good name.
It's always well to keep a name of this character.

RONDON
Camaradas?

They all murmur protests in a polyglot of lan-
guages.

RONDON
Perhaps you prefer Rio Teddy?

Roosevelt roars out a laugh.

ROOSEVELT
Anything but that!

As Simplicio and Paishon hammer the post into
the ground, we see on its side the carved letters
"RIO ROOSEVELT.

73

RONDON
Three cheers!

He leads the camaradas in lusty cheers for Roosevelt. After:

ROOSEVELT
I propose three cheers for Brazil!

All do so heartily.

ROOSEVELT
Three cheers for Colonel Rondon!

These cheers ring out.

EXT. ANOTHER PART OF THE RIVER - DAY

Raybeams of light from the late afternoon sun grid the river as the boats pull in to shore for the night.

LATER - THE RIVERBANK

Machetes swing, clearing a space for the camp.

LATER STILL

The camp is set up. While the others bustle about, Roosevelt sits at a small table, writing.

ROOSEVELT (V.O.)
We already felt the need for fresh meat.

EXT. JUNGLE - DAY

ON TREETOP

The HAUNTING SOUND of an owllike bird call echoes.
 PAN DOWN to Kermit and Luiz, standing in an open stretch of ground with only a tall MOUND OF EARTH in the center.

KERMIT
Cotinga?

Luiz nods. Again the bird CALLS. Kermit shoulders his rifle, gestures to Luiz that he'll circle around. Luiz nods and Kermit heads into the jungle.

INTERCUT KERMIT AND LUIZ

Kermit stalks through the growth, the COTINGA'S CALL loud, haunting--

Luiz is now standing just in front of the mound. He looks at it curiously. It towers higher than his head. Kermit cocks his rifle.

Luiz hears a GUNSHOT. The cotinga sound suddenly ceases.

Kermit struggles through the dense vegetation, trying to spot the fallen bird.

Stops. Something he sees--or doesn't--makes him frown.

Luiz is surrounded by silence. It unnerves him. He hears a RUSTLING movement

LUIZ
Bwana Dandy?

Nothing. He grows more nervous. The fronds of a palm stir at jungle's edge, but no one appears. Anxious, Luiz steps back--and stumbles over a vine--

Kermit finds his bird, lying dead on the ground--

A SHATTERING CRY--human--

SECONDS LATER

Kermit runs toward where he left Luiz. Another
CRY--

Kermit rushes out of the jungle thicket and sees
Luiz--

His face and arms are entirely covered by RED
ANTS storming out of the mound--their home.

Kermit rushes forward, tries to brush the atta-
cking hordes off Luiz. The camarada SCREAMS-
-red bites already cover his visage.

In knocking away the ants, Kermit also suffers.

A new wave of marauders sally forth from the
mound--

Kermit grabs Luiz by the shoulder, pushes him
forward.

The humans flee the scene of battle.

EXT. CAMPSITE - NIGHT

Luiz's face is a ravage of tiny wounds. Dr. Cajazeira is administering salve. Luiz shivers from

fever. Nearby, Rondon is in mid-anecdote--The expedition leaders are all gathered around. It's war story time. Kermit smokes his pipe, lounges. Cherrie busies himself with specimens.

RONDON
Half of us were naked and the other half looked like bloody rags, you could hardly tell skin from cloth, but the worst, the absolute worst--

LYRA
--were the Berni flies.

RONDON
They burrow into your skin. You have to cross-cut gashes and squeeze them out but if you're too exhausted-

LYRA
They stay awhile.

RONDON
The fires of hell cannot be worse.

LYRA
And this after a month of eating nothing but Brazil nuts.

KERMIT
I saw none on the trees this afternoon. That's odd, isn't it?

RONDON
(a beat, exchanging a
look with Lyra)
It's very rare for the crop to fail.

LYRA
  (brusquely, to Kermit)
You don't know where to look.

AT THE RIVER

Simplicio, fishing with two other camaradas,
pulls up a line from the water. The hook is empty. Simplicio looks worried.

SIMPLICIO
No fish.

CAMPSITE

it's Cherrie's turn to tell a tale.

CHERRIE
In the Venezuelan insurgence we found our-
selves trapped in an open plain. There we were,
five naturalists and a taxidermist, and bearing
down on us at full gallop, thirty horsemen. We
fired till our hands burnt, killed the first line,
then the second, but they kept charging with
those long lances. Fearsome weapon, a lance,
when it's coming straight at your eyes. The man
next to me, SPLAT, split his head open like a
ripe melon. Finally we had to shoot their horses,
terrible waste of fine animals. Stallions, all of
them, purebred. I stuffed one and took him
home to Vermont.

Dr. Cajazeira, having finished with Luiz, joins the group. In b.g. Luiz is trembling, looks ill.

DR. CAJAZEIRA
He has fever. Bad.

RONDON
He will not be the last.

Roosevelt watches Luiz, reflecting. Remembering.

ROOSEVELT
Gentlemen, I'm no stranger to jungles.

FLASHBACK

EXT. JUNGLE MUCK - CUBA - DAY

A HISSING SOUND, sinister as sudden death.

Leaves, thick jungle leaves, shake dank diseased water as a MAUSER PROJECTILE, source of the HISS, zips through and finds its target,

A ROUGH RIDER

crouching as best he can behind a thin canopy of leaves. THUNK! the bullet burying itself in his chest, he falls face down, instantly dead, his distinctive khaki uniform merging with a stagnant pool of brown mud.

ROOSEVELT
Blast!

Eyeing the body sunk in mud and slime, he almost gnashes his teeth. Roosevelt seems ready
to explode. He strides like a lion mad with rage
through this swamp, past more bodies of his regiment, past the lucky remainder hunkered
down in mud and stench vegetation.

His dress makes a conspicuous target: blue shirt
and yellow suspenders, a cocked khaki hat.

Only one sergeant, BUCKY O'NEILL, follows his
leader's example and braves the bullets without
crouching for cover.

ROOSEVELT
Be ready to move, boys.

O'NEILL
What are our orders, Colonel?

ROOSEVELT
Kill the enemy!

O'NEILL
Hard to do when you're sittin' like a duck.

ROOSEVELT
Blast these generals!

He slaps his horsewhip against his thigh, eyes
his horse stirring restlessly nearby, doesn't even

flinch when a Mauser bullet THWOCKS a tree trunk beside his face.

A LIEUTENANT is belly-down beside O'Neill.

LIEUTENANT
I'll say this for Teddy, he's got guts.

O'Neill lights a cigarette, smiles.

O'NEILL
He's like me. The Spanish bullet isn't made that'll kill me.

There is a high-pitched WHINE. A Mauser bullet, passing through O'Neill's mouth, blasts a gaping hole in the back of his head.

A MEDIC rushes to him, but--

O'Neill's body has hardly hit the ground when Roosevelt is in the saddle.

ROOSEVELT
Forward march!

A SHOUT from the Rough Riders. They leap out of this rancid hellhole to follow their leader.

Even the medic. O'Neill's body is left where it lies.

All now is a blur of images of brown khaki, splashing water, bodies hurtling through clouds of steam mist.

A VISTA opens.

We exit the jungle onto the FIELD OF BATTLE where a U.S. cavalry regiment is pinned down, giving and receiving fire from a fortified Spanish position above on KETTLE HILL.

Roosevelt doesn't stop.

FLASHCUTS of startled cavalrymen.

A CAPTAIN, hunched down with his men, stands up waving as if to bar their advance.

ROOSEVELT
Why are you lying on your bellies?

CAPTAIN
We're waiting orders.

ROOSEVELT
I am the ranking officer here. Advance!

CAPTAIN
Sir, unless the general--

ROOSEVELT
Then let us through, sir!

He spurs past. The Rough Riders follow, firing volleys at the Spanish entrenchments above.

SERIES OF SHOTS

The fire and fury of the charge--

Roosevelt pulling his revolver, firing--ignoring the Rough Rider hit just beside him, his head EXPLODING from a Mauser's impact.

Men falling, firing, smoke rising from the intense gunfire--

Startled BLACK CAVALRYMEN of the 9th Regiment, having just finished tearing down a barbed wire barrier, jumping aside to let the Rough Riders through, shouting encouragement.

A bullet POPPING cloth from Roosevelt's elbow, him ignoring it like a fly, firing, always waving his men forward.

Roosevelt plunging across a stream, mounting the hill.

ANOTHER BARBED WIRE FENCE

this one intact. Roosevelt leaps off his horse, climbs over the fence in one motion, begins to run.

A SMALL HACIENDA

atop Kettle hill serves as the Spanish fortification.

Roosevelt runs toward it, firing. Bullets WHIZ beside him. Some of his men, struggling to keep up, are hit, fall.

POV FROM HACIENDA

A madman, all gnashing teeth and spectacles and hat curled back at the brim, is charging toward them, seeming to pull by main rage a killing hailstorm of gunfire.

The madman fires--

A SPANISH SOLDIER falls in FRAME.

ANOTHER ANGLE

The Spanish flee the hacienda. Roosevelt leads a barrage of fire. They are cut down mercilessly.

KETTLE HILL

as Roosevelt reaches the crest. In a blur of seconds, he sees the hacienda is empty, all the enemy dead.

The hill is theirs.

Still too seething to relish the victory, Roosevelt immediately reconnoiters.

Across the way another battle rages, the situation the same as before, American soldiers entrenched below. Trapped.

ROOSEVELT
San Juan Hill. If we can take that--

As fast as he's arrived at hilltop, Roosevelt leaves it, starting to run toward San Juan Hill.

He stops after a few paces. Turns, looks back. All the Rough Riders are clustered on Kettle Hill.

ROOSEVELT
What, are you cowards?

LIEUTENANT
We're waiting for the command.

Roosevelt smiles.

ROOSEVELT
Forward march!

SHOUTING, the men storm down from the height to join him. Each rank of American cavalry and infantrymen greet them with CHEERS, then forsake their bellies to join the charge.

POV FROM KETTLE HILL

Roosevelt and the Rough Riders lead a gathering WAVE.

The air fills with gunsmoke and the sound of
THOUSANDS OF THROATS.

When they reach the summit of San Juan Hill, a
jubilant HURRAH rolls like a thunderclap across
the lowland where, against all odds and conven-
tional military strategy, Roosevelt has led this
charge to victory.

EXT. TRENCH BIVOUAC - DAY

Two weeks later. A grim Roosevelt walks through
a stinking, rain-puddle encampment. Everywhere he looks he sees soldiers coughing, feverish, or dead--just their feet protruding from
under mud-crusted blankets. Even in death,
they are not spared the circling, buzzing mosquitoes.

ROOSEVELT
Intolerable! These men have got to be sent home!

The lieutenant accompanies Roosevelt.

LIEUTENANT
Sir, the War Department--

ROOSEVELT
Blast the War Department! I'll draft a letter to
the press.

EXT. CUBAN SEAPORT - DAY

Roosevelt, himself a picture of robust good
health, watches as one after another of his
proud Rough Riders are lifted on palettes onto a
cargo ship. The rest of his troops, hardly better
off, straggle behind.

ROOSEVELT (V.O.)
That great army. We won the war, and there we
were in full retreat--

BACK TO PRESENT

as Roosevelt SLAPS DEAD a mosquito feasting
on the blood of his forearm.

ROOSEVELT
--from a bunch of insects!

He leans back. Story over. Now it's Kermit's
turn. All eyes turn to him.

Kermit shifts uncomfortably. Hard to match
these harrowing stories of adventure, but one
has to try. He removes his pipe.

KERMIT
I'll never forget what an
ordeal it was--
(clearing his throat)
freshman hazing at Harvard.

EXT. JUNGLE - NIGHT

From a POV as of a spectator some distance
away, we see the men gathered around the
campfire, breaking out into LAUGHTER. Then
MOVING BACK, until the campfire is a tiny
flame. And the SOUNDS OF THE JUNGLE take
over. Wild, savage sounds of animals and insects, at farthest remove from the small enclave
of humans who have intruded into their world.

EXT. CAMP - DAY

Dawnlight breaking--

 ROOSEVELT

stirs awake, sits up, dangles his legs over his
cot. Kermit also awakes, sits up from his palette
bed on the ground.

ROOSEVELT
Sleep well?

Kermit nods yes.

KERMIT
You?

ROOSEVELT
I had capital slumbers. Deep and profound.

KERMIT
You missed dinner.

Kermit points at Roosevelt's legs. His father
looks down, notes with a start that the calves of
his bloomer underpants have been eaten away.
Shreds at knee level show where the depredators
left off.

ROOSEVELT
Termites?

Kermit breaks out into laughter at the sight of
the legless bloomers. Roosevelt
huffs.

EXT. RIVERBANK - DAY

The feverish Luiz is lifted into a balsa by two
camaradas.

EXT. ON THE RIVER - LATER THAT DAY

SERIES OF POV'S

from the boats on the river, which winds
through lush low-lying marshland, past submerged trees--a swamp here, the vegetation
creating a canopy. Caymans scurry on the
banks.

ROOSEVELT (V.O.)
The broad, deep, placid stream bent and curved in every direction. We were still wholly unable to tell where we were going or what lay ahead of us.

The tropical sun beats down as the boats navigate a placid stretch. Roosevelt mops his brow. Beads of sweat fall from his face, DRIP DRIP into the water.

Paishon barks an order at Julio, who has been slacking off paddling. Julio joins in paddling and they bring the balsa abreast of Kermit and Dr. Cajazeira's boat. Dr. Cajazeira seems to be nodding off in the heat. Roosevelt takes a spare paddle, BANGS it on the side of his boat. Dr. Cajazeira startles awake as Roosevelt laughs.

ROOSEVELT
Sooner me than a piranha, doctor!

Their boat moves ahead. Dr. Cajazeira smiles at Roosevelt's caper, turns to Kermit.

DR. CAJAZEIRA
I marvel at your father. Where does he find such energy?

KERMIT
Inside.
(a beat, musing)
His mother died the same day my stepsister Alice was born. One hour later, so did her mo-ther-- father's first wife. People say they'd never seen a man so broken. He went West to the Bad-lands. Some days he never left the saddle. Bliz-zards, sandstorms, Indians. Dared them to kill him. Wanted it. But they couldn't. And it was like he buried the past so deep--he'd been crazy mad in love with his wife, but it's been 30 years, and he's never uttered her name again. Not even to his daughter. Their daughter.

DR. CAJAZEIRA
Extraordinary.

He looks over at Roosevelt who is regarding the trees at bankside, some of which lean far into the river.

INTERCUT

Cherrie notes that Julio is nodding off.

DR. CAJAZEIRA
(to Kermit)
What was her name?

Before Kermit can answer, Simplicio SHOUTS.

A rumbling ROAR--

CHERRIE
Julio!

Kermit stands up in his dugout to look--

A BOULDER rises just above water level--

Julio jerks awake too late to notice it in time and
Roosevelt's boat strikes head on. The balsa spins
on its axis, begins to tip over.

As the men on board SHOUT, Julio and Paishon
strain against paddles, trying to right the boat
back into the main current and away from the
whirlpool around the boulder. In vain.

Roosevelt impulsively leaps out of the boat.

CHERRIE
Colonel!

Standing waist high in the water, Roosevelt
pushes against the balsa, trying to dislodge it.

As Kermit passes in the other boat, its paddlers
working furiously to keep the boat away from

the boulder, he jumps out beside his father. They strain against the balsa--

ROOSEVELT
Heave-ho!

Muscles strain. The balsa budges, tips right side up.

A wave of released water roars against Kermit and Roosevelt who struggle to hold footing. Roosevelt's leg is CRUNCHED against the boulder. Blood spurts.

The other boats approach. Rondon is standing in the prow of his--

HIS POV

up ahead the river funnels between low rocky crags, forming fearsome rapids.

Rondon shouts an order. All the rowers strain toward shore.

THE BALSA

floats away. Roosevelt lunges toward it, grabs a boat paddle extended by Cherrie.
Paishon reaches down, grabs Kermit. Cherrie pulls Roosevelt aboard. He lies on his back in the boat, gasping from exertion.

AT THE BANK - MOMENTS LATER

the balsa pulls in to join the others.

ROOSEVELT
By gosh, that was fun!

Dr. Cajazeira spots Roosevelt's wounded leg as
he steps out of the boat.

DR. CAJAZEIRA
I'll treat that.

ROOSEVELT
Nonsense.

Insects are already BUZZING around the wound.

ROOSEVELT
My friends are enjoying themselves too much.

EXT. ON SHORE ABOVE RAPIDS - DAY

The expedition members are gathered on the
rocks, looking down where the river runs like a
millrace through a narrow chute created by gra-
nite rock abutting from both riverbanks.

ROOSEVELT
I've never seen such a wide river compress itself
like this.

JULIO
(mutters)
Devil river.

THE PORTAGE - SERIES OF SHOTS

--The camaradas wield axes like scythes, felling trees.
--Rondon stands on a rise, surveying the best route for the portage, pointing to Paishon where to begin to cut a trail.
--Paishon directs the camaradas in trailblazing.
--A multitude of blades chop the fallen tree branches and trunks into 1-meter sections.
--The log sections are laid down over the trail, forming a washboard road.
--The camaradas carry gear and provisions on their shoulders over the trail.
--The now-empty boats are pushed and dragged over the log sections. It is real labor. Men strain at it.

ROOSEVELT

joins with Paishon to help carry Luiz. When Paishon starts to protest--

ROOSEVELT
J'insiste, j'insiste. I'm old but brawny.

They start along the trail behind the boat-bearers.

ROOSEVELT
You boys know the poetry of François Villon?

Paishon and Luiz shake their heads.

ROOSEVELT
Appalling man but a delightful poet. We'll pass
the time with Villon.

He begins to recite a Villon poem. Luiz is not so
ill as not to look utterly incredulous.

CHERRIE

stands on the riverbank. Spotting something on
the ground, he leans down, picks it up. Rolls it
in his palm.

KERMIT, RONDON AND LYRA

are standing together. Cherrie comes up, shows
Kermit what he's found: a desiccated Brazil nut.

CHERRIE
Brazil nut, or what's left of it. I've yet to find
a fresh one.

LYRA
Keep looking.

Cherrie bristles, but before he can respond they
all notice that Kermit is shaking.

KERMIT
Malaria. I've had it since I was a kid.

Kermit doesn't miss that Lyra is aghast.

KERMIT
I live with it.

He moves past him to join the camaradas in portaging his dugout.

LATER - ROCKY CRAG OVERLOOKING RIVER

Kermit, clearly suffering, helps carry his heavy dugout over a narrow section of trail.

EXT. RIVER - PORTAGE END - DAY

Kermit's boat is the last one portaged. When it is deposited on terra firma, Kermit slumps to the ground, exhausted, breathing heavily.

Lyra, who has helped with the portage and looks none the worse for it, mutters to Dr. Cajazeira:

LYRA
He won't make it.

EXT. CAMPSITE - NIGHT

A cloudburst drenches camp and campers. The camaradas, mostly in hammocks, suffer through sheets of water tumbling from the trees. The campers on the ground are suffused in water and mud.

KERMIT

is lying in an ever increasing puddle of water. Shivering. Unable to sleep. Kermit looks toward his father. Roosevelt sleeps on his cot, above the pools forming below.

A cloud bursts. Kermit shakes uncontrollably as the swamp rises around him.

EXT. BANK - THE DUGOUT CANOES - NIGHT

Waves of water burst against the boats' moorings. One suddenly breaks free, floats into the river current and is rapidly submerged.

DAYBREAK

Roosevelt and Rondon watch as Lyra wades into the river, reaches a portion of carved wood lodged against a driftwood tree--the broken prow of the lost boat.

SERIES OF SHOTS

--A tree plummets to earth, felled by the camaradas' axes.

--Branches are lopped off.

--Bark chipped.

--With as much precision as they can manage, the camaradas begin to carve and hew the tree trunk into dugout shape.

ANGLE ON THE FEET OF THE CAMARADAS

being constantly attacked by ants, swollen horribly.

Kermit circulates among the camaradas, offering them cigarettes for morale.

KERMIT
Tabac?

Pedrinho smiles, takes one gratefully.

Julio is lounging under a tree, loafing. He signals to Kermit who shakes his head no.

KERMIT
No work, no smoke.

Despite this reproof, Julio still makes no move to get up and join the others. Paishon glares at him, looks as if he's had enough of Julio's shirking.

MOMENTS LATER - ANGLE ON LONG
WHIPLIKE BRANCH

as Paishon snaps off a last leaf, leaving a cord of flexible but firm hard wood. He moves over to Julio, who looks up, mutters a curse when he realizes what Paishon intends to do.

Paishon begins to hammer blows around Julio's head and shoulders. Again and again. Julio tries to ward off the shocks with his arms, to little effect.

Finally Paishon stops.

PAISHON
You work or we leave you!

He turns on his heel. Julio glares at him, blood on his face, hate in his eyes.

THAT NIGHT

under candlelight the work goes on.

Roosevelt is at a small portable table, writing.

ROOSEVELT (V.O.)
It was not pleasant to have to stop. With our limited supply of food and no knowledge whatever of what was ahead of us, it was important to make good time.

Roosevelt's PEN scratches across the paper.

ROOSEVELT (V.O.)
But there was no alternative.

Roosevelt pauses, gathering his thoughts. Something attracts his attention--a SHAPE reflected on the palm tree trunk in front of him from candles held by the toiling camaradas.

The shape flickers, wavers, assumes a human form--a WOMAN'S.

FLASHCUT

a tear-stained paper, a raging pen writing "My life has been lived out," then furiously BLOTTING OUT the rest.

BACK TO:

ROOSEVELT'S PEN

has fallen from his hand, rests on the paper. Roosevelt is staring at the tree trunk, shocked. The camaradas holding the candles shift position. The light shape vanishes.

Roosevelt blinks, the spell broken--but still looks stunned by what he has seen or thought he has seen.

CAMPSITE - THAT NIGHT

Rondon sleeps but stirs restlessly.

RONDON
(talking in sleep)
No, leave me alone !

A SHADOW

looms over him. Ominous, sinister--sways a little. Rondon murmurs in his sleep.

HIS NIGHTMARE

A row of emaciated, exhausted men trek through
the forest, Rondon in the lead. Feet virtually
bare, what shoes they have are in tatters or re-
duced to a web of threads. Their bodies are
masses of welts.

VOICE (O.S.)
Coronel...meu Coronel.

Rondon, himself a wreck, hardly has the
strength to turn.

RONDON
Who is it?

VOICE (O.S.)
Help me. Help me.

WHAT RONDON SEES

is a man clad in ragged shorts, worn down almost to a skeleton--the man we have seen in the beginning, except now

HIS HEAD is that of a GROTESQUE INSECT. The monster FALLS FORWARD--onto Rondon who opens his eyes in shock and terror as THE BODY LANDS ON HIM.

Rondon YELLS, rolls off his cot, realizes then it is not the monster of his nightmare, but KERMIT, out of his head with fever.

Rondon just stares as Kermit struggles to his feet, gives him an uncomprehending look, lurches away.

MATCH CUT TO MORNING

Kermit standing with evident difficulty, trembling, but dressed and determined as Roosevelt, Rondon and Lyra debate.

LYRA
He was delirious all night!

KERMIT
I feel fine. I'm over the worst.

RONDON
(troubled)
It might be better if--

ROOSEVELT
Colonel, he'll hold his weight. When I was a child
I battled asthma and licked it. Kermit's got to do
the same.

Rondon thinks a moment, then nods. Lyra
storms off.
Rondon and Roosevelt turn, move away together.
Rondon is pensive, reflecting.

RONDON
On my last trip, there was this man. We found
him wandering in the jungle, lost. A skeleton. He
should have been dead long before. The men
said he was the devil. He kept calling me like a
little child, wanting me to save him. But I could
do nothing. We didn't even have the strength to
bury him. Now, ever since we're on this river, I
see him in my dreams. What is he trying to tell
me?

ROOSEVELT
Every leader of men suffers casualties. Forget it.
Remember, you're a Positivist.

RONDON
Yes, when my eyes are open

EXT. RIVER - DAY

One of the new canoes is slid down the bank
into the water. It floats buoyantly. Antonio is
waiting knee-deep in the water. He shakes the

canoe from side to side, testing its balance. After
a moment, to Rondon:

ANTONIO
Good.

ROOSEVELT
Maybe it will change our luck.

ANTONIO
I know rivers like fish. Bad waters ahead.

EXT. RAPIDS - DAY

Churning, boiling--Antonio was right.

The boats rest in an eddy at bankside, everyone grimly eying what lies ahead.

KERMIT
It looks calmer on the left.

LYRA
You're dreaming.

KERMIT
(very sharply for him)
It's worth a reconnoiter.

No compromise likely, they look to Rondon and Roosevelt for resolution.

ROOSEVELT
(to Rondon)
Colonel, are you thinking what I'm thinking?

RONDON
Our progress has been so very slow, it's necessary to risk.

MOMENTS LATER

Kermit's lead canoe on the water, approaching a small spit of land in the middle of the current. Kermit barks an order in Portuguese. The boat veers left.

MOVING with the boat, sharing the tension as the passengers anxiously look ahead, we see--

rapids. Kermit directs the paddlers to head toward shore, but he has hardly said it when--

A WHIRLPOOL

catches the boat, spins it around. It swirls backward toward the rapids. Kermit yells. Simplicio and Antonio paddle furiously to no effect.

A FALL

an abrupt drop-off unseen until now. The boat goes over, splinters on the rocks below, ejecting the three men.

SERIES OF SHOTS

Antonio quickly surfaces, swims hard, finds the shore.

Simplicio struggles against the raging current, goes under.

Kermit is caught in mid-river, hurled downstream despite his efforts to break out. He fights to stay above water--just manages to dodge a protruding boulder.

Roosevelt runs along the riverbank, searching the rapids that have swallowed his son.

Kermit fights for his life, propelled like a cork through the wild waters.

A BRANCH

stretches out from the bank. With what remains of his strength Kermit reaches, grabs it, arresting his plunge toward death.

Kermit clings to it, gasping for breath, exhausted.

EXT. ON SHORE - DAY

Camaradas scout the banks, peering over the river. Others wade in shallow water, searching.

Rondon, Roosevelt, Kermit and Lyra are standing on shore watching. Paishon comes out of the water, hands Rondon what he has found: a SPLINTERED PADDLE.

RONDON
That's all?
(Paishon nods)
Keep looking.

LYRA
(to Kermit)
His blood is in the river. You will taste it when you drink. It will burn your heart.

KERMIT
There was nothing we could do.

LYRA
You killed him!

Kermit punches him to the ground. Lyra gets
up, smiling.

LYRA
You struck first. I'm released from duty.

He hits Kermit, sending him falling backward
into a side stream. Lyra plunges in, punches
Kermit again. Cherrie starts to intervene. Roosevelt stops him with a hand on his arm.

ROOSEVELT
Let them settle it.

CHERRIE
He's weak from fever and--

ROOSEVELT
It's their business. Let's take care of ours.

Roosevelt turns on heel, strides away as if he
doesn't care to see the outcome. Rondon though
taken aback follows suit. Dr. Cajazeira also. Finally Cherrie does the same.

KERMIT AND LYRA

Their fight has taken them downstream. Kermit
summons strength, lands a few blows but Lyra
gains the upper hand, pummels him with blow

after blow, sending him back to where the stream enters the deep jungle.

Lyra pauses to let Kermit struggle to his feet.

LYRA
You want me to stop?

KERMIT
Fuck you.

Lyra hits him again.

LYRA
Go back to your tea rooms and salons.

Kermit rips off a driftwood branch, brandishes the sharp pointed end like a spear. Lyra is startled, flinches as Kermit thrusts--

--past Lyra--

Into the gaping mouth of a CAYMAN. The massive jaws, intending to scissor Lyra from behind, instead CRUNCH the wood.

Lyra stumbles back onto the bank, away from the cayman which thrashes its tail furiously, gnawing its unpalatable prey.

Kermit clambers onto the bank with Lyra.

LYRA
It can reach us here.

He pulls Kermit up and away with him seconds before--

THE CAYMAN'S GAPING JAWS SLAM INTO FRAME, biting nothing but air and mud bank.

Kermit and Lyra watch as the angry cayman slides slowly back down through the mud.

LATER - NEAR THE BANK

Kermit is swabbing the blood from his face, using a small pocket mirror set on a tree branch.

Roosevelt comes up.

KERMIT
Same old story. Some day maybe I'll win a fight.

ROOSEVELT
Don't bellyache! You got whipped, that's all. Pick yourself up off the floor with your chin up.

KERMIT
Yes sir.

Roosevelt nods with a snap of the head. Lesson learned.

ROOSEVELT
Try this.

He gives Kermit a handful of a Vaseline-like substance.

ROOSEVELT
Dr. Cajazeira says it's tops for bumps and
bruises.
(hands it to Kermit)
And if you do win a fight some day, don't gloat.

EXT. NEAR THE RIVER BANK - DAY

ANGLE ON POST

as with his hunting knife Kermit carves an inscription: "IN THESE RAPIDS DIED
POOR SIMPLICIO."

Kermit regards it for a moment, then hands it to
Paishon.

MOMENTS LATER

Paishon hammers it into the ground beside the
river. All the expedition members stand beside it,
heads bowed.

Kermit regards the post with particular feeling.

SOME TIME LATER

everyone is standing by the canoes.

RONDON
Our best chance is to unhook the balsas. If the
first boat doesn't make it, the next will have to
shift course. Fast. Paishon, you and Lyra will
take the lead boat.

He moves away, leaving Kermit to reflect on this
demotion. He looks at his father, but Roosevelt
turns away.

EXT. IN THE RAPIDS - DAY

The boats ride big chutes, taking water but ma-
naging the worst of it. The lead canoe with Lyra
is already through.

Kermit's boat goes through next.

Roosevelt rides with Cherrie in the rear. Ahead
they see the new canoe, Antonio and Pedrinho
aboard, already waterlogged.

ROOSEVELT
We chose a big strong tree, good. Bad--it has all
the buoyancy of last year's cement.

HERRIE
Bail, Pedrinho, bail!

Too late. The boat ships sideways, SLAMS into a
boulder. Wood snaps. In a moment the canoe is
gone.

In passing, Cherrie manages to grasp Pedrinho's hand, haul him aboard. But Antonio is too far away. He gasps, swallows water, flounders.

Roosevelt frantically uncoils rope at his feet, flings it back toward Antonio, who is just able to grab it. Roosevelt reels him in through the maelstrom, but the rope lodges against his injured leg. Blood flows afresh.

Roosevelt grimaces from the pain.

EXT. NEAR CAMPSITE - DAY

ANGLE ON PALM TREE TOP

its leafy branches swaying a bit, but not from wind. Paishon pokes his head up through the leaves. He unstraps a machete from his thigh and CHOPS.

EXT. CAMPSITE - DAY

Paishon and other camaradas drop the PALM TREE TOPS they have cut into a boiling pot where the cook works.

LYRA

is scribbling calculations while Rondon watches.

LYRA
We lost a third of what's left of our provisions, a rifle, the rope and pulleys--portaging will be harder--the spare aneroid--

CHERRIE
--and two canoes.

Roosevelt is wrapping his bloody leg. Dr. Cajazeira watches, concerned.

DR. CAJAZEIRA
Twice in three days. Bad luck.

ROOSEVELT
My Achilles leg. I broke it in a trolley accident a few years ago.
(pats it)
Leave it to our hungry friends. Our fever patients need you.

He points to a good ten or so camaradas who look wan, listless in b.g. The doctor nods, moves over to see to them.

Kermit, sitting beside his father, watches the doctor.

KERMIT
When I was a kid I hated quinine. Still do.

The cook brings over the dish. He ladles out bowlfuls. Everyone eyes the gooey green purée.

DR. CAJAZEIRA
Palm buds.

ROOSEVELT
Well, if you're going to eat something that's neither tasty nor nutritious, they'll do fine.

Cherrie holds up a stewed frond.

CHERRIE
They go better with Brazil nuts.

RONDON
(to Kermit and Cherrie)
You were right, gentlemen. The crop has failed.

KERMIT
I spotted a monkey as we came in. How does it taste?

LYRA
When you're starving? Guess.

Kermit stands, shoulders his rifle.

KERMIT
Wish me luck.

He starts toward the jungle but Lyra stands as if to bar him from going.

LYRA
It's nearly dark. We can't afford to lose a man.

KERMIT
Even me?

He brushes brusquely past Lyra, heads toward
the jungle.

IN THE JUNGLE - MOVING WITH KERMIT

scanning the treetops above, brushing aside
thick foliage, heading deeper into the primeval.

ANGLE ON MONKEY

leaping from treetop to treetop.

PAN TO KERMIT

he starts to run in pursuit. PAN TO LYRA--he's
followed.

ON THE RUN WITH KERMIT

he pounds through thick vegetation, a mud bog,
always keeps the monkey in sight.

Lyra, following, huffs and pants, surprised by
Kermit's endurance and single-minded pursuit.

Suddenly Lyra runs full force into a tree branch,
comes away with a faceful of WASPS. He yells,
falls to beating them off.

KERMIT

reaches a vantage point. He is sweating profusely, gasping, but coolly raises the rifle.

The monkey is crouched to leap from one tree to
another, does so--

Kermit's shot hits him in mid-arc.

The monkey bounces off a branch, lands O.S--
we HEAR a SPLASH.

KERMIT
Shit!

He runs through the thick jungle, breaks
through to see

A RIVER AFFLUENT

the swift current carrying away the body of the
monkey.

Kermit starts running along the bank after it.

LYRA

comes out onto the bank upstream, sees Kermit
on the run

LYRA
No!

Kermit doesn't hear, disappears around a curve. Lyra looks up at the sky. It is full of ominous rain clouds. He curses, runs in pursuit of Kermit.

KERMIT

sees the monkey sinking below the surface. Without slacking pace, he drops rifle and dives in.

IN THE STREAM - BELOW SURFACE

Kermit angles down toward the bottom, the water clear enough for him to spot the sinking carcass. Kermit grabs the monkey's leg.

A HUGE SHAPE

stirs the thick mud at stream bottom--a MASSIVE PARAIBA CATFISH, almost three meters long. The monster fish opens its GAPING JAWS, rises up into the current toward Kermit.

Kermit's eyes widen. He turns, swims frantically. The fish easily closes the gap. The enormous mouth closes onto Kermit just as he heads for air.

ON THE SURFACE

the monkey carcass goes tumbling over a cascade, followed by Kermit who lands in swift water. Kermit gasps air.

He swims furiously toward the bank, looking behind him for sign of the catfish.

LYRA

comes running out of the jungle to the bank bordering the cascade. He searches the stream below for Kermit--nothing.
 The silence here is complete, profound, disturbing.

THUMP! Lyra JUMPS, startled as something drops to the ground beside him.

The DEAD MONKEY.

Lyra turns. It's

Kermit--soaked, leg bloody, but smiling.

KERMIT
How do you like your monkey?

Before Lyra can answer, RAIN DROPS begin to spatter their faces.

LYRA
If we live to eat it--rare.

ANGLE ON STORM CLOUDS

Bursting--

EXT. JUNGLE - DAY

Lyra and Kermit make their way through a whiteout of stormrain.

Lyra looks lost. The rain begins to fall even harder.

Lyra motions to Kermit to follow him. He heads toward a giant pacova palm whose roots stretch above the ground.

Kermit follows Lyra who squeezes between the massive roots.

INT. ROOT SHELTER - DAY

Utterly drenched, Kermit and Lyra find dry conditions here. Lyra wrings out his shirt and hair. Kermit eyes the alcove.

LYRA
We have to wait for light. Even if by miracle I find the way, for the animals it's dinnertime. You understand?

Kermit nods. He is staring at something behind Lyra. Something that gives him pause.

LYRA
You can sleep standing up?

Kermit is too nervous to speak. HIS POV: HUN-
DREDS OF SPIDERS, not small either. They
crawl everywhere in, around and among the
huge roots--not to mention the two men.

One particularly large spider starts to head up
Kermit's leg. He kicks it off in horror and revul-
sion. Lyra gasps, grabs Kermit's arm.

LYRA
Don't provoke them! Their bite is lethal!

KERMIT
(quietly, all apprehension)
What am I supposed to do?

LYRA
Stand still. Make them think you're part of the
tree.

Watching the horde of arachnids swarming at
his feet, it is clear Kermit will have a hard time
doing so.

KERMIT
Spiders scare the everlasting hell out of me. I
can't be a root, much less a tree.

Lyra reflects a moment. Pulls something out of
his pocket, gives them to Kermit.

LYRA
Chew these.

KERMIT
Cocoa leaves.

LYRA
You will feel much better.

Another spider begins to crawl up Kermit's leg.
He begins to chew a cocoa leaf with extreme ar-
dor.

TIME CUT

Lyra and Kermit are overrun.

LYRA
I come from a village so poor we used to eat insects and be happy for it. I was 15 before I knew
what it was like not to be hungry. When Colonel
Rondon fed me fresh beef from Argentina, it was
so good I cried. He knew I would work with him.
He knew that no matter what hell we went
through, I'd never complain.

Kermit is trying desperately to maintain aplomb
as the spider host swarm over legs, arms,
shoulders.

LYRA
What is it like to be rich? To be able to buy anything you want whenever you want?

KERMIT
Pretty damn good.

LYRA
I thought so.

KERMIT
(grimacing as a spider crosses his neck)
Right now I'll give you a thousand bucks for
another cocoa leaf.

Lyra slowly--so as not to agitate his own spi-
ders--pulls other cocoa leaves out of his pocket.

TIME CUT

Under the influence of the cocoa leaves, Kermit
and Lyra are beginning to loosen up.

KERMIT
My father never treated us like privileged rich
kids. Every summer we went to his ranch in
South Dakota and worked till our hands bled.
That's how I learned to use rope. If I had to lasso
one of these creepy crawlers, I could. Oh God--

He eyes his crotch. There's movement inside,
but it isn't from Kermit.

LYRA
They like it there. It's warm. Cocoa leaf?

KERMIT
(and he really means it)
Please.

EXT. RIVER CAMPSITE - DAY

Roosevelt sits with Rondon, watching the relent-
less rain.

ROOSEVELT
He's going to be married when we return. The
fear that something might happen to him is a
continual nightmare. I don't think I could bear
to bring bad tidings to his mother and his betro-
thed.

RONDON
They'll have found shelter somewhere. Does your
son have any special fear of spiders?

INT. ROOT SHELTER - KERMIT AND LYRA -
DAY

The rain has stopped. Kermit and Lyra feel no
pain now.

LYRA
"Bye-and-bye?" What is this "bye-and-bye?"

KERMIT
The future.

LYRA
You say hello to the future, not bye-bye.

KERMIT
No, see, what it means is, in the time to come--
woo, there's one right on my head, must weigh
three pounds!

They break out in giggles.

KERMIT
I'm going to name him Charlie, Charlie Chaplin.

LYRA
Who?

KERMIT
My uncle.

He giggles. Lyra has to giggle too, though he
doesn't know why or care.

KERMIT
Come on, let's do it.

LYRA
All right, I'm ready.

KERMIT
You remember the words?

LYRA
After 50 times?
(more giggles)

KERMIT
All right, all right--

KERMIT AND LYRA
(singing together)
"I wonder if ever a cowboy/Will be seen in those
days long to come/I wonder if ever an Indian/
Will be seen in that far bye-and-bye."

Two small human voices rise in song as outside
the rain keeps pouring down.

EXT.JUNGLE - DAY

ankle-deep pools, moisture everywhere.

ANGLE ON LIANA VINE

as Lyra slashes it open with his knife. Fresh water pours out as from a hose. Lyra takes long
draughts. Kermit sloshes up behind him. With
difficulty he raises his boot, quicksanded in the
viscous mud. Kermit looks exhausted and frustrated by the effort to walk in this swamp. He
removes his boots, tosses them into the ooze. He
has the dead monkey strapped to his back.
Lyra hands the liana vine to Kermit, who drinks.

LYRA
Careful of the bees.

Lyra points at Kermit's feet.

KERMIT
Bees that live in the mud? This time you are joking.

EXT. CAMPFIRE - NIGHT

The carcass of the monkey rests on the spit
where it has been gratefully roasted.

ROOSEVELT (V.O.)
The flesh gave each of us a few mouthfuls. How
little it took to cheer us!

All the expedition members are eating morsels.
Roosevelt swallows a bite, gets up from beside
the campfire, moves past Kermit, slaps him on
the back in gratitude and relief.
Kermit is swabbing a salve on his feet, pricked
by dozens of bee stings. He looks at Lyra, who
just smiles and shrugs. He wasn't joking.

ROOSEVELT
Our prehistoric ancestors dined on simians
many a night. We haven't come so very far.

He sits down so Dr. Cajazeira can treat his leg.

RONDON
(to Kermit)
What you saw was the paraiba. A catfish. The
natives fear it more than the cayman because it

lurks on the river bottom, in mud where they cannot see it.

LYRA
The biggest ones can swallow a man whole.

RONDON
Marvelous eating though.

KERMIT
Next time I'll carry a worm.

ROOSEVELT
Man-eating catfish. Good Lord, what next? 6-foot tadpoles?

Dr. Cajazeira is examining Roosevelt's leg. He looks worried.

DR. CAJAZEIRA
You've developed an abscess. That's why your fever's mounting.

Roosevelt chooses not to respond.

CHERRIE
When I get home, I'm going to treat myself to griddle cakes and maple syrup.

KERMIT
Me, strawberries and cream.

They look to Roosevelt.

ROOSEVELT
A mutton chop, with a tail to it.

CHERRIE
I make my own syrup. Have an orchard of maple trees, around 1200. My hired hand Fred Rice'll be commencing to tap them right about now.

ROOSEVELT
There's nothing like a northern spring. I remember one, I was just twenty-two, I--

He stops abruptly, riveted by a VISION floating before him, just outside the firelight : a beautiful YOUNG WOMAN (ALICE LEE), in the white blouse and long dress characteristic of the late 19th century. She looks ready for a springtime carriage ride.

Roosevelt knows her name, but has not deigned to say it for 30 years, and he doesn't say it now. He just stares, rendered speechless by a beauty which made men's heads spin. His most of all.

Kermit, Cherrie and the others don't know what to make of this sudden silence.

THE APPARITION

wafts away into the depths of the jungle forest.
Roosevelt snaps, not easily, out of his vision.

ROOSEVELT
Nostalgia. Foolish at a time like this.

He stands up despite his injured leg, moves
away from the ministrations of the startled Dr.
Cajazeira.

EXT. A SET OF FIERCE RAPIDS - DAY

rushing with frightening force.

PANNING FROM RAPIDS

to the expedition fighting its way through the
jungle up a rocky slope.

SERIES OF SHOTS

--The dugouts being dragged over another wa-
shboard macheted out of the dense jungle.
--Bruised swollen feet of the limping camaradas.
--Heads and arms flayed by branches and
thorns.
--Insects biting and stinging.
--Weary muscles straining.

THAT NIGHT - ANGLE ON TORCHES

being rammed into holes in the earth, one after the other, quick movements, fire SEARING THE GROUND WITH FLAME.

Kermit has a blazing torch which he wields like a spear, WHOOSH WHOOSH above the ground, battling the invaders. The others rush over to help, defending with a wall of fire.

THEIR ATTACKERS are a column of FORAGING FIRE ANTS.

ROOSEVELT (V.O.)
The very pathetic myth of beneficent nature could not deceive even the least wise being if once he saw for himself the iron cruelty of life in the tropics. Nature is entirely ruthless, entirely indifferent to good or evil, and works out her ends or no ends with utter disregard for pain or woe.

WHOOSH! The flames beat back the marauders.

EXT. RIVERBANK - DAY

Roosevelt sits writing over a small folding table. He wears headnet and gloves as protection against a fearful horde of insects BUZZING, HUMMING and SCREECHING around him.

Roosevelt's visage can hardly be seen through the headnet, only the glasses, 2 STEAMY ORBS. He scratches in the margin of his manuscript--

INSERT - A SQUIGGLY LINE

ROOSEVELT (V.O.)
This is not written very clearly. My temperature is 105.

EXT. PORTAGE TRAIL - DAY

Roosevelt limps on his injured leg, gasps as he tries to follow the trail and keep up with the camaradas. He is feverish, sick. Nevertheless he carries a box of provisions.

He stops for breath. Dr. Cajazeira comes up.

DR. CAJAZEIRA
Mr. Roosevelt, please, let me.
        (indicating the box)

ROOSEVELT
Imagine the conquistadors. They barged through this landscape in heavy mail and armor. Reprehensible characters, just freebooters, enemies of art and native cultures. Still, you have to admire such determination.

He shoulders the box of provisions, again starts on the trail. Dr. Cajazeira watches him huff and puff.

DR. CAJAZEIRA
Indeed.

EXT. CLIFF ABOVE RIVER - DAY

Kermit, aided by Lyra, lowers a canoe down a cliff to calm water below a set of rapids.

When done Kermit hauls up the rope. He has a thought. He looks hard at the rope as it coils up in his hands.

EXT. CAMPSITE BESIDE RIVER - DAY

All sorts of GEAR, from food to clothes to miscel-
laneous, are being tossed on a pile willy-nilly.

ROOSEVELT (V.O.)
We had already cut out all comforts. Now we cut
to the bone.

Cherrie brings over a box, puts it on a pile.

DR. CAJAZEIRA
What's that?

CHERRIE
Various species of tanager. And a crested blue-
bird. Audubon would never forgive me.

RONDON

looks up from his own winnowing when his DOG
suddenly bolts into the jungle.

RONDON
Lobo!

The dog doesn't respond to his command. Rondon exchanges looks with Lyra.

RONDON
He senses something.

Rondon shoulders his rifle.

ROOSEVELT

is rifling through a duffel. He fishes out the last
contents: a pair of new gray shorts and the Oxford Book of French Verse.

Roosevelt thinks a moment, weighing both items
in a separate hand. He makes the choice, places
the book of poetry on a small pile of essentials.
He looks around.

HIS POV

the effects of the long wearying days are obvious
now. Most of the men are stripped to shorts,
have not bothered to wash, limp on swollen feet,
are marked by cuts and bruises. Paishon's
shorts are torn, ragged. Roosevelt proffers his.

ROOSEVELT
How about it, Paishon? Straight from Abercrombie & Fitch.

Paishon nods yes, smiles thanks as he takes
them.

Kermit is admiring his silk suit. He notes Lyra
regarding him.

KERMIT
My celebration suit. I wore it our last day in
Africa. Wanted to wear it when we came off the
river.

He shrugs, tosses it on the discard pile. He
moves away, leaving Lyra in FRAME.

EXT. JUNGLE - DAY

ANGLE ON A POOL OF WATER

still, stagnant. In b.g. Rondon and Lobo move
through the jungle. HOLD a BEAT.

O.S. we HEAR a SPLASH. The water in FRAME
swirls, ripples from the movement of someone or
something O.S.

LOBO

smells the presence, growls, runs off in its direction.

Rondon tenses, raises his rifle, bolts in a shell,
moves forward slowly.

MOVING WITH RONDON through the still silent
jungle. Moisture dripping from the trees, insects
devouring a palm frond--something SPLASHES.

Rondon hisses, calling the dog. No movement in
response. Rondon edges forward slowly.

PANNING HIS POV

nothing but pristine jungle, but as PAN ENDS, Rondon senses something, turns--

LOBO

is impaled against a tree trunk, a spear jammed through his throat.

The sound of VOICES BEGINS TO ECHO.

Rondon fires WARNING SHOTS in the air. The voices stop.

Rondon cocks the rifle, edges away--tense, nervous.

EXT. AT THE RIVER - DAY

ON SPEAR

as the expedition leaders examine it.

ROOSEVELT
Recognize it?

Rondon shakes his head.

VOICES again begin to ECHO from the jungle. Rondon raises his rifle, wary.

RONDON
They've undoubtedly never seen a white man.
They're curious.

LYRA
Friendly?

RONDON
(shouting toward the voices)
Come out! We mean no harm!

No response. Just more VOICES echoing to each
other.

LATER THAT NIGHT

THE JUNGLE

dark, sinister, somber, is still ECHOING to the
sound of the Indians' voices.

PANNING THE MEN--most are feverish; some
are trying to sleep with little success as the
voices RESOUND from one part of the jungle to
the other--an uncanny effect.

The healthier camaradas are posted as guards,
with rifles and knives ready. They look scared
and nervous.Rondon paces angrily, casting looks
of rage at the jungle. He passes Julio, who is fast
asleep despite the fact he's on guard duty. Rondon elbows him.

Julio stirs awake, grunts, but when Rondon moves away, he promptly nods off again.

ROOSEVELT

lies on his cot, tossing and turning with fever. Cherrie sits beside him, jotting notes in a journal. Kermit regards his father.

KERMIT
I've never seen him so helpless.

Cherrie reflects on this a moment, then scribbles a remark in his journal.

 INSERT - CHERRIE'S WORDS

"It is doubtful if all our party ever reaches Manaus."

Kermit gets up, moves over to the edge of the jungle.

ON ROOSEVELT

his eyes suddenly open. He looks toward the jungle. He hears the sound of a WOMAN SOBBING. Loud, poignant.

Cherrie is writing, turned away from Roosevelt, does not remark his movement.

Kermit starts to take a piss. In midstream, listening to the voices, he has a thought. He raises his nozzle, sends pee on a high arc toward the unseen neighbors.

Immediately he hears what sounds like A CURSE, then rustling vegetation as someone flees.

Pedrinho, one of the guards, starts to move after the intruder but Kermit holds him back.

Rondon stalks over, takes the gun from Pedrinho.

Roosevelt dangles his feet over the hammock, steps down, takes a pace toward the jungle, toward the sound of the sobbing--but a RIFLE SHOT snaps him out of his dream vision.

Rondon SHOWERS A FUSILLADE toward the jungle, blasting leaves and trees and everything else in the path of the bullets. Rondon doesn't stop until he's emptied the rifle.

LYRA
Why did you do that?

RONDON
For me.

Rondon unleashes a defiant SHOUT, screams a challenge in Indian dialect.

After a moment of silence, the VOICES RE-SUME.

Roosevelt has come up beside Rondon.

ROOSEVELT
Colonel, if they'll kill a good dog, they won't spare an American president.

MOMENTS LATER

The boats are launched into the river.

EXT. ON THE RIVER - NIGHT

The boats edge through darkness eerily lit by the moon. The VOICES pursue them, ECHOING from bank to bank.

The boats are filled with nervous men--disquiet, apprehension evident on their faces.

Roosevelt turns angry. Fever or no, he stirs, sits up from where he's lying on a makeshift pallet.

ROOSEVELT
What we need is a good ghost story. Have you heard the one about Carothers and the haunted castle?

His listeners don't know whether to be shocked or amused, all except Kermit. He smiles.

ROOSEVELT
(spinning the tale)
A hunter by trade, Carothers was no believer in
the supernatural.

Kermit lights up his pipe, leans back in the boat.

ROOSEVELT
But something about the castle he'd just inheri-
ted unnerved him. He'd heard the tale of the
maiden who walked the ramparts, and of the
bone-chilling wind that--

Kermit gestures and Roosevelt stops. They all
listen.

The VOICES have stopped.

KERMIT
(very softly)
Guess they haven't heard this one.

Roosevelt smiles, resumes.

ROOSEVELT
(raising his voice for the Indians)
That wind from the frozen north that went
WHOOO! WHOOOO!

EXT. RAPIDS - DAY

A chasm through which the squeezed river descends.

AT THE RIVERBANK

Lyra and Rondon are conferring. Lyra grabs a
canteen, takes a long swig of water.

LYRA
This ridge continues--like you see. Very steep
and rocky. We can manage the boats but it will
take time.

RONDON
With the Indians behind us? I'd rather chance
the rapids.

LYRA
If we head for the chute on the right--

NEARBY

what's left of the provisions rests in the leaders'
dugouts. While they're conferring some distance
away, A HAND reaches into a rucksack, pulls
out a piece of food.

PAISHON (O.S.)
Stealing food.

JULIO

the thief caught in the act, whirls, confronts Paishon.

PAISHON
We miss food. No surprise now. You never hungry. No surprise.

JULIO
You kill us! We work, die for nothing in jungle!
Devil jungle!

Paishon hammers Julio to the ground with a powerful fist to the jaw. When Julio starts to get up Paishon hits him again.

Paishon moves in for more but Julio gets up, flees.

Paishon starts to follow but Julio is already gone.

ANGLE ON RIFLE

lifted from where it rests in a canoe near where Dr. Cajazeira is lancing and draining the abscesses on Roosevelt's leg. Insects buzz and hum around the wound. Roosevelt grimaces.

DR. CAJAZEIRA
It will not heal until we find better conditions.

ROOSEVELT
(a beat)
The odds are against me coming out. Aren't they?

Before Dr. Cajazeira can reply HEAR a RIFLE SHOT.

ANGLE ON PEDRINHO

running--

AT THE RIVER

he comes upon Roosevelt and Dr. Cajazeira He is anguished, shocked.

PEDRINHO
Julio has killed Paishon!

DR. CAJAZEIRA
It's not possible.

PEDRINHO
Yes! He run jungle!

Roosevelt struggles to his feet. Enraged.

ROOSEVELT
Where?

Pedrinho points--

Roosevelt picks up a rifle, heads that way before the astonished Dr. Cajazeira can stop him.

He limps badly.

IN THE JUNGLE - MOVING WITH ROOSEVELT

hunting Julio, rifle at the ready. Roosevelt spots
a man moving past a palm. He runs after him,
giving no quarter to his fever.

INTERCUT ROOSEVELT AND JULIO

Roosevelt comes to a stop. Breathing heavily,
hard.

The run has fogged up his glasses. He tries to
wipe them clean. He HEARS A MOVEMENT.
Hastily replaces them. Roosevelt squints.

HIS POV

everything is vague, cloudy through the steamy
lenses.

JULIO'S POV

is of Roosevelt peering around like a man half-
blind. Julio raises his rifle, aims--

Roosevelt spins, looks all around, still sees no-
thing--but with a sixth sense--he suddenly
wheels, FIRES A SUCCESSION OF SHOTS. A
tree trunk is BLASTED.

Roosevelt runs forward, stops beside the tree, finds JULIO'S RIFLE, dropped when the shots panicked him and made him flee.

EXT. CAMPSITE - DAY

Paishon's body is lying beside the food sack. Rondon and the camaradas are standing above.

ANTONIO
Paishon fell forward on his hands and knees. His ghost will follow Julio as long as he lives. Julio will never be free.

SERIES OF SHOTS

--The camaradas dig a grave with axes and knives.
--The body is laid in the grave. Earth heaped over.
--All the expedition members stand watching with bowed heads. Roosevelt notes the shorts he has given Paishon as the earth covers them.
--Roosevelt places a rude cross at the head of the grave.

ROOSEVELT
For a gallant soldier of Brazil.

--Rifles fire a volley in memory of Paishon.
--FEET turn, move away from the lonely grave.

EXT. CAMPSITE - NIGHT

In mid-gorge, hammocks are slung at the foot of
a cliff on a narrow boulder-covered slope. Roosevelt's cot sags now like a broken-backed centi-
pede.

GUARDS

camaradas with rifles, stand watch over the
sleepers.

Pedrinho is one. Pacing slowly in the darkness,
he suddenly thinks he hears a sound. He comes
alert, cocks his rifle. After a moment:

PEDRINHO
Julio?

Nothing moves or responds. Pedrinho remains
tense.

EXT. GORGE RAPIDS - DAY

the first canoe comes through into placid water.

LATER - ON THE RIVER

Roosevelt's balsa trails Rondon's and the other
canoes.

CHERRIE
I hardly think we'll meet worse obstacles than
that.

ROOSEVELT
If we do, we're finished.

INT. JUNGLE - DAY

Julio runs panic-stricken through the jungle.
His face is feverish, but as he stops to catch his
breath, it seems there is something else frightening him. He hears a SOUND, as if something or
someone is moving through the jungle toward
him.

FLASHCUT

a pair of legs wearing Roosevelt's shorts, walking
through the forest.

Julio gasps, turns and runs.

ON THE RIVER

Roosevelt's boat is nearest when Julio runs out
of the brush and onto the bank.

JULIO
Surrender! Surrender!

Everyone in the boat looks to Roosevelt for orders.

ROOSEVELT
Don't stop.

Julio watches the boats pass, astonished. He hears a SOUND behind him. He turns in fright--

EXT. ON THE BANK DOWNRIVER - DAY

The boats being tied up--Roosevelt and Rondon confer.

RONDON
I saw him, but you are the chief of this expedition. I wanted to consult with you first.

ROOSEVELT
I had no intention of taking him aboard and jeopardizing the rest of the men. They're sick and weak and to add constant guard to their lot-- only if you told me as a superior officer of the army and responsible to the laws of Brazil that it's a duty.

RONDON
That is my view.

ROOSEVELT
Then you must do as your sense of duty demands.

Rondon nods to Pedrinho and Luiz.

RONDON
Take rifles. Go back and look for him.

Cherrie mutters, furious at this decision.

RONDON
(ignoring Cherrie, to Pedrinho and Luiz)
We'll wait for your return.

They head back down toward the river. Rondon
moves away. Cherrie paces.

CHERRIE
Folly! Inconceivable folly!

ROOSEVELT
Cherrie, you're wasting valuable energy.

Kermit tosses Cherrie a rifle.

KERMIT
Go shoot a rare bird.

EXT. HEART OF THE JUNGLE - DAY

Julio is running, fleeing his unseen pursuer. He
stops in a clearing. Looks around, sees no one,
hears nothing. He relaxes.

But suddenly he realizes where he is.

SERIES OF SHOTS:

red ants, a snake coiling around a tree branch, flies biting him, insects crawling over his feet. Most of all the IMMENSE, SILENT, TRACKLESS FOREST.

VOICES begin to echo from the forest--Indians.

Panic.

Julio SCREAMS-

SHOT—the jungle. The sound ECHOES in the heart of its vastness.

ROOSEVELT (V.O.)
Julio was never found.

EXT. ON THE RIVER - DAY

The boats float down a stretch of calm water.

Cherrie is looking over a map.

CHERRIE
By my calculation, we've come about 125 kilo-
meters.
(to Rondon)
How much farther do we have to go?

RONDON
I can only guess. Maybe 5 times that.

ROOSEVELT
Well, a river normally describes a parabola in its
course. The steepest descent is in the upper
part. Let's hope in the future we won't encounter
so many and such difficult rapids.

ANOTHER ANGLE

As the boats disappear around a bend--

ROOSEVELT (V.O.)
It was a hope destined to failure.

ACT THREE

SUPER: APRIL 2, 1914

SERIES OF SHOTS

--Two camaradas lie stricken in their canoe from fever.
--The broiling sun beats down.
--Roosevelt lies propped against a load of gear.

ROOSEVELT (V.O.)
We had been exactly a month going through an uninterrupted succession of rapids.

HIS POV

a succession of hills pass (SERIES OF DIS-
SOLVES).

ROOSEVELT (V.O.)
Half rations had sunk to quarter rations.

CUTTING BETWEEN BOATS

RONDON
(to Lyra in the next boat)
The aneroid says we are descending. By all logic
we should be entering a plain.

Roosevelt looks wan, weak.

ROOSEVELT
(murmuring softly)
"In Xanadu did Kubla Khan a stately pleasure
dome decree."

Cherrie is writing in his journal.

CHERRIE (V.O.)
Our strength and courage alike are nearly exhausted.

Lyra regards the two ill camaradas.

LYRA
Joaquin and Marisco can no longer work.
(a beat)
Very soon some of us will begin to die.

Rondon's visage is grim. A VOICE rings in his
ears:

VOICE (O.S.)
Meu Coronel! Meu Coronel!

ROOSEVELT
"--through caverns measureless to man--"

He looks down, into the flowing water which, for
once, reflects sunshine. Stares. Rapt by fever
and remembrance.

THE WATER

glistens and sparkles with silver, a translucent
effect which takes Roosevelt into THE PAST.

EXT. OYSTER BAY - DAY

another boat, another time, though the sunlight
seems to create the same effect in this johnboat
where a divinely beautiful woman reclines, the
young ALICE LEE ROOSEVELT.

ALICE LEE
Will you always love me, Theodore?

ROOSEVELT (O.S.)
Always and forever.

ALICE LEE
There are so many things you want to do. But I
only have you.

She leans back into the shimmering sunlight.

ALICE LEE
Love me always.

This scrim begins to break up, and Alice Lee to disappear, and in a moment we are

BACK TO PRESENT

realizing along with Roosevelt that the apparition has vanished because the RIVER CURRENT has become swifter.

HEAR A LOW ROAR

Roosevelt snaps out of his reverie, studies the current for an instant. Raises up. Cherrie pauses in his writing.

ROOSEVELT
It's going to canyon.

Cherrie looks uncomprehending.

ROOSEVELT
"Canyon!"

EXT. CANYON GORGE - DAY

And that it does.The River of Doubt plunges in massive chutes of turbulent rapids through a high, narrow canyon--certain destruction for any dugout canoe. TALL CLIFFS rise sheer above the river.

`EXT. CLIFFTOP ABOVE RIVER - DAY

Kermit, Lyra and Rondon scramble up the rocky ridge above the cliffs. Far below we see the River of Doubt cascading between the canyon walls.

AT THE TOP

all of them pause, gasping.

THEIR POV

the river extends as far as they can see through hills. Rondon slowly scans the horizon. Grimly.

EXT. CAMPSITE - DAY

as Rondon, Lyra and Kermit return from their scout, all the others regard their faces for some hopeful sign. There is none. Rondon moves over to Roosevelt.

RONDON
Colonel, I--

ROOSEVELT
Spit it out. No faint hearts here.

Rondon nods, turns to the others.

RONDON
It's a very hard climb along the cliff. Very hard.
We can manage the loads. But the boats will ne-
ver make it.

ROOSEVELT
You're sure?

KERMIT
Impossible, even if we were healthy.

Silence as this sinks in. But Roosevelt, even
deathly ill, is no man to tolerate indecision.

ROOSEVELT
Colonel Rondon, the orders of the day, sir.

Rondon turns, walks a few paces.

RONDON
We'll have to abandon the canoes. Every man
must fight for himself through the jungle.

Roosevelt looks grim, the others stunned. Lyra
and Kermit just look at the ground. Cherrie is
angry.

CHERRIE
That's practically a death warrant. Just look
around.
(indicating fever sufferers)
They're so out of their heads they'll go in circles.

RONDON
Between all of us, some will find their way. To
civilization and home.

CHERRIE
You're dreaming. That jungle will eat us alive,
one by one. It's only a question of who holds out
the longest.

LYRA
And if we stick together, what then? We can't
carry litters.

CHERRIE
Well, that's calling a spade a spade, isn't it?

ROOSEVELT
A man who looks for favors has no business
making an expedition like this. I'm only a bur-
den. Kermit, you and Cherrie go on. I'll stop
here.

Kermit looks stunned but doesn't hesitate.

KERMIT
No sir, I'm not leaving you to die in this jungle.

ROOSEVELT
Son, let's accept the ugly facts.

KERMIT
Since when have you ever done that?

ROOSEVELT
Since--

He can't go one. His eyes widen as if the fever has seized him, or he sees a vision that over-comes him. He totters--Kermit grabs him before he falls to the ground.

He and Cherrie carry Roosevelt away.

RONDON
(bitterly)
This river is cursed.

He moves away, leaving the group to their thoughts.

EXT. ROOSEVELT'S CAMP SPOT - NIGHT

Roosevelt tosses and turns on his cot, delirious with fever. Cherrie watches over him, writing in his journal. He pauses as Roosevelt mumbles something incoherent. Kermit comes up. Cherrie shakes his head.

CHERRIE
He feels so responsible for us all. It's nobody's fault. Sometimes Nature wins.

Roosevelt abruptly sits up on his cot.

ROOSEVELT
Cherrie! Cherrie!

CHERRIE
Yes sir.

ROOSEVELT
Did you have a good dinner tonight?

Kermit and Cherrie exchange looks.

KERMIT
Yes father. We all had a fine dinner.

Kermit looks down at their 2 bowls of mushy
palm tree soup.

ROOSEVELT
Good, good. I don't need much, but you boys
need strength.

Roosevelt lies back, still mumbling verses.

ROOSEVELT
"In Xanadu did Kubla Khan a stately pleasure
dome decree. In Xanadu did Kubla Khan--"

CHERRIE
I don't believe he can live through the night.

Kermit slumps to a seat beside his father, devas-
tated.

LYRA AND RONDON

are stuffing bags with what remains of their
possessions. Lyra pauses a moment, reflects.
Then to Rondon:

LYRA
It has been a great honor to serve with you. You
gave me a life.

RONDON
I'm no savior.

Stricken, he moves away.

KERMIT

watches his father lying on his makeshift pal-
lette of palm fronds, raving deliriously with fever.

KERMIT
He loves poetry. Songs. Whatever's good senti-
ment in whatever language. To him they're not
just words. He's never understood why a certain
lackadaisical son can't recite whole verses off the
top of his head, like he can.

He looks up at the night sky. Stars are shining
but rain clouds are beginning once again to scud
across.

KERMIT
I know some. If he should--
(choking up a little)
Kipling : "He scarce had need to doff his pride,
Or slough the dress of earth."

CLOUDS begin to blot out the stars.

KERMIT

"E'en as he trod that day to God, So walked he from his birth, In simpleness and gentleness and honor--"

The rain begins to fall in sheets, another torrent.

EXT. CANYON ENTRANCE - NIGHT

A man walks along the river bank to where the river plunges into the canyon depths. It's

KERMIT

as the torrential rain pours down, Kermit doesn't move, except to raise a fist and shake it in silent rage at the barrier which has blocked the expedition.

EXT. ROOSEVELT'S CAMPSITE - NIGHT

MUCH LATER

the rain has stopped. Cherrie sleeps, exhausted.

Roosevelt stirs awake, hearing the sound of a WOMAN SOBBING.

Roosevelt gets off his cot, moves toward the jungle. Cherrie doesn't stir.

THE SKY

clears off, revealing a full moon.

IN THE JUNGLE WITH ROOSEVELT

the moon shadows create an eerie effect, coming and going as brief clouds pass. Roosevelt moves through this spectral forest toward the source of the haunting WAILING.

He spots a figure in white. Moves toward it. It is a WOMAN, her back to him, shoulders shaking from her weeping.

As Roosevelt approaches she turns, startling him to a halt. He recognizes her tear-stained face.

Roosevelt tries to say a name. The words don't form.

A cloud blots the moon. She disappears in the darkness. When the light comes again she is gone.

ROOSEVELT
No! No!

ALICE LEE (O.S.)
Theodore.Theodore.

He looks around desperately, sees her white form moving through the jungle. He runs after her.

EXT. CAMPSITE - DAY (DAWN)

Kermit arrives back, immediately realizes some-thing is wrong because an object rests in the mud in front of his eyes--his father's cot, collap-sed and broken at last.

In the dimness he sees footprints in the mud. Kermit grabs his rifle, runs off to find his father.

INTERCUT ROOSEVELT AND KERMIT

Roosevelt ignores the tangled vines which fre-quently block his path, bulls his way through, pursuing the white wraith.
 He comes to a clearing where a backwater of the river forms a swampy lowland.

She is standing some distance away from the bank, hovering on the surface of the water.

ALICE LEE
Do you recognize me, Theodore?

ROOSEVELT
Yes.

ALICE LEE
I've changed.

ROOSEVELT
No.You're just as beautiful as--
    (hesitating, too moved)

ALICE LEE
You forgot me, Theodore. Laid me in the cold
ground to rot in the rain. I loved you with all my
heart. And you forgot me.

ROOSEVELT
I had to live!

The wraith turns her back on Roosevelt, SOB-
BING again. She starts to waft away.

ROOSEVELT
No!

He plunges into the water after her.

Kermit runs through the jungle, following the
tracks. His injured feet LEAVE BLOOD.

Kermit loses the trail, the tracks disappearing in
a mass of green growth. He looks around, frantic. Spins on his heel.

KERMIT
Father!

The cry ECHOES in the treetops.

Roosevelt is plunging through the swamp water, crossing toward a small island, chasing the crying phantom.

In a treetop just ahead, a MONKEY looks down curiously at the desperate man.

As Roosevelt scrambles, his injured leg SCRAPES against a jagged piece of driftwood.

BLOOD streams from the wound across the surface of the water.

ALICE LEE
Goodbye, Theodore.

Roosevelt bursts thirty years of silence:

ROOSEVELT
Alice! Alice! Alice!

Kermit hears the cries.

The wraith stops, turns back. Roosevelt smiles.

His blood suffuses the water. Rapid movements begin crisscrossing the stream. PIRANHA.

Roosevelt approaches the wraith. She smiles, extends her hand.

The piranha rush toward their prey.

Roosevelt reaches out his hand.

A SHOT rings out.

The MONKEY FALLS into the water behind Roosevelt. The piranha swerve, attack it. Flesh is riven, gulped.

Kermit plunges into the water after his father.

Roosevelt is shocked as the specter suddenly disappears.

Kermit fires another shot at the carcass of the monkey. The bullet expunges a chunk of flesh and blood. Their blood lust fueled, the piranha attack with insatiable fury.

Kermit reaches his father, grabs and hustles him toward a spit of land close by.

ROOSEVELT
Alice! Alice!

He SCREAMS in pain as a piranha attacks his leg, a moment before Kermit manages to pull him onto the bank.

Kermit knocks the cannibal fish off Roosevelt's leg, then beats it to death with the rifle butt. Other piranha SLAM into the bank in frustrated rage.

Roosevelt could care less. He is looking toward the jungle in anguish.

ROOSEVELT
Come back! Alice, please God, come back!

KERMIT
Father. Father!

Kermit struggles to hold his father back.

KERMIT
She wants you to die!

This startles Roosevelt. He stops.

ROOSEVELT
What?

KERMIT
She hates you! Don't follow her. Goddammit, I
need you!

Roosevelt turns toward his son, stares at him for
a long moment as if regaining lucidity.

ROOSEVELT
She can't leave me again, she can't!

He struggles to get up. Kermit swings the rifle
butt against his head, knocking him out cold.

Kermit grimaces at the blood on his father's
head. He takes out a cloth handkerchief from his
pocket, wets it in the stream, swabs the wound.

LATER

Roosevelt is conscious, but he says nothing, stares toward the jungle where the phantom disappeared. Kermit decides to break the silence.

KERMIT
You remember all the times I was sick? Weak, whining. You'd take me out on the terrace at Sagamore Hill and make me look around. At the world. Then you'd recite, "Life is sweet, brother. There's day and night, brother, sun, moon and stars and--"
(pretending to forget)
and-

ROOSEVELT
"And a wind on the heath. And likewise a wind on the heath!"

Roosevelt revives, to Kermit's relief.

ROOSEVELT
Blast it, boy, verse is written to be remembered.

KERMIT
Yes sir.

Roosevelt thinks a long moment.

ROOSEVELT
She was the fairest flower that ever blew. I dreamed all my dreams for her. Thought that if I lived every minute of my life hard enough and fast enough, I could outrun memory.
(a beat)
Son, I love your mother.

KERMIT
   (softly)
I know.

Roosevelt nods. Starts to get to his feet. Kermit
helps him.

EXT. CAMPSITE - DAY

In FRAME, the dugout boats, moored at the
bank. Emptied now of all gear and provisions,
they look a little forlorn. Kermit is standing next
to them, thinking.

Lyra comes into FRAME with Rondon.

LYRA
What shall we do with the boats?

RONDON
(a beat)
Leave them for luckier men.

He has a PACK. All the other members of the expedition are gathered on shore with what personal gear they can carry, waiting before heading
into the jungle for the last of their bedraggled,
beaten party--ROOSEVELT--to hobble into their
midst.

RONDON
I have no idea where we are or which direction to
take. Your guess being as good as mine, you're
free to go where you wish.

He waits for comment. When there's none immediately forthcoming:

RONDON
May God guide you well. Better than me.

He straps the pack onto his back, but before he
can take a step--

KERMIT

suddenly turns--

KERMIT
(loudly, emphatically)
No!

He strides back to the group of leaders.

KERMIT
We can't abandon the boats. They're our only
chance.

Everyone exchanges looks--the objection comes
from such an unlikely source.

LYRA
Don't you understand? That's our problem. That
canyon. What would you have us do, Bwana
Dandy? Fly?

Rondon makes a despairing gesture toward the raging torrent of whitewater entering the canyon.

RONDON
Even the fish must fear that.

Kermit doesn't back down. It's a different man who answers.

KERMIT
(fiercely determined)
By God, I'll get us through.

SERIES OF SHOTS

--Kermit clambering onto a rock at rapids' edge where he can scan through binoculars the cliff downriver.
--Ropes being coiled and lashed.
--Kermit showing Pedrinho how to fashion a knot.
--Rope slung around neck and shoulders, Kermit leading the camaradas up the precipitous cliff above the river canyon.

EXT. CLIFFTOP - DAY

Kermit ties a rope around his waist in rappel position, Roosevelt and Rondon at his side. When it's done--

RONDON
Godspeed.

ROOSEVELT
If you find yourself marooned--

KERMIT
I won't. I've got a rendezvous in Madrid.

Roosevelt--holding back emotion with effort--
gives his son a bear hug. Steps back.

Kermit turns, steps into space, rappelling down
the side of the cliff toward a small slab of bank,
sufficient for footing, on the river beyond the
impassable stretch of rapids.

EXT. ON THE BANK - DAY

hitting ground, Kermit quickly unties the knot,
sends the rope back up, signals for Lyra and
Cherrie and the two camaradas above to begin
descending.

EXT. CAMPSITE - DAY

Pedrinho fashions a rope knot to tie around the
first canoe.

EXT. CANYON EDGE - LATER THAT DAY

The canoe is being slowly let down via ropes by
the remaining healthy camaradas through the

first set of rapids, down canyon to where Kermit and the others wait.

INTERCUT

Now on the wild water, the canoe bobs like a cork.

Kermit wades as far as he can into the river to retrieve it.

Cherrie stands on the bank with a rifle, guarding against the unexpected.

Just as Kermit reaches out to grab the canoe's tether--

THE KNOT SLIPS

Unfettered, the canoe rips away, tosses and turns at the mercy of the rapids, SHATTERS to bits against a cliff wall.

Kermit and the others react grimly.

LATER

This time it's Kermit making the knot. He ties the Indian spear that killed Lobo to a canoe prow.

ON RIVER - A SHORT TIME LATER

As the canoe surges downstream Kermit--standing kneedeep in water near the
bank--FLICKS A LARIAT across the river.

The loop coils over the spear--

Kermit pulls it fast. With Lyra and the camaradas' help, he hauls the canoe out of the current.

LATER

All the canoes now rest together on the bank. Kermit connects the lead canoe to a rope wound around his waist. He loops it over his shoulder, begins to move along the face of the cliff. A second rope is strapped to his waist. There are very narrow finger holds and toeholds Kermit can use. It is slippery, touch and go to the maximum.

Lyra, Cherrie and the camaradas watch.

IN MID-LEDGE

now much higher above the river, Kermit looks down, sees a row of spike-edged driftwood awaiting him should he fall. As bad luck would have it, he almost does, slipping--grabbing onto a ledge and holding on by his fingernails. His feet dangle above the deathtrap.

Sweating, flailing, grimacing, Kermit manages to regain his footing. He takes a deep breath.

So do Lyra, Cherrie and the camaradas.

MOMENTS LATER

Kermit descends to a wider stretch of bank, signals--

Lyra jumps into the rushing torrent. He tumbles, rolls, tries to hold up his arms.

A LASSO

spins out from the bank, lands around his arms and shoulders. Lyra grabs it. Kermit hauls him to the bank.

SOME TIME LATER

Kermit and Lyra rein in the first boat, which has been lowered via rope harness through the current by the others upstream. Kermit anchors it, signals for the others.

EXT. CLIFFTOP - DAY (SUNSET)

The remainder of the expedition are portaging the loads over the rugged edge of the cliff. It is hard going.

Roosevelt walks very slowly, Dr. Cajazeira by his side. He is clearly in pain.

He stops, panting for air.

Rondon comes over. Dr. Cajazeira takes his arm. Roosevelt waves off their concern.

ROOSEVELT
I'm all right, blast it.
　　(a beat)
Some sunset, eh? A sweet thing, a sunset.

He takes a deep breath, begins again his laborious ascent.

PANNING FROM TRAIL

Down below the river continues its tortuous route through the canyon.

A BOAT

the last one in this stage, suddenly RIPS out of one of the camaradas' hands. The others, unable to hold it under the pressure of current, let the rope slip.

Cherrie goes falling backward, bangs his head against a rock. The rifle slung around his shoulder falls in the sand.

The canoe does not career far before it lodges against a boulder. But the weight of water spilling over its bow threatens to sink it.

Kermit and Lyra and the camaradas rush into the current. They reach the boat, start to right it.

KERMIT
Push!

They do with a heave. The boat turns right side up.

A CAYMAN

launches off the opposite bank toward them.

Cherrie sits up, stares around, groggy.

INTERCUT ACTION

The crew with great difficulty and expense of strength head the boat toward shore, losing some ground against the current. They all see the cayman at the same time.

KERMIT
Hurry!

Lyra detaches from the group, sloshes against current to the bank, runs toward Cherrie. When

Lyra reaches Cherrie he grabs, unslings the rifle. The barrel is choked with mud.

The cayman closes in.

Kermit draws his knife strapped to his waist.

Lyra FIRES. Chunks of sand are ejected with the bullet.

WHAM! The shot hits the cayman. It doesn't faze the monster. Lyra curses, tries to empty the gunbarrel of debris.

The camaradas abandon the boat, scurry toward shore.

KERMIT
Save the boat!

He shoves it toward them. The camaradas with the grit to do so grab it, haul it toward shore.

WHAM! Another shot into the thick hide. No apparent effect, the cayman still coming.

Kermit sees the whites of the cayman's eyes. Brandishing the knife and nothing else, the man they called Bwana Dandy turns to face the beast. Alone.

The cayman surges toward him, massive jaws opening.

Kermit leaps, dodging the SNAP of the massive head, in the same motion rolls onto the cayman's back, jabbing the knife into the massive hide, seeking a vulnerable spot. The cayman rolls, roiling the water.

Lyra hesitates, curses in frustration--too much tumbling to get off a good shot.

POV UNDERWATER-from here we can see just how massive the cayman is. Too big. Kermit's puny knife goes plummeting, wrenched out of his hand by the twisting cayman.

Kermit gets footing in shallower water, stumbles back.

The cayman charges. Kermit won't make it.

LYRA'S EYE

Sights--

WHAM! This shot hits as the cayman slams into Kermit--and hits home. Kermit grabs the now useless jaws, rolls the giant over onto its back, shoves it into the current. The body floats downstream.

MOMENTS LATER - ON THE BANK

The camaradas push the boat safely onto the mud bank. Nearby Lyra helps Cherrie to a seat on the sand. Kermit comes up, collapses beside them.

CHERRIE
Rather big specimen.

KERMIT
It wasn't robin redbreast.

Kermit gives Lyra a look which says all for gratitude.

EXT. ROCKY SLOPE - NIGHT

Kermit, Lyra and Cherrie and the camaradas are scrunched up in the rocks, a slim purchase on terra firma indeed.

EXT. CLIFFTOP CAMPSITE - DAY

While the camaradas here sleep, Dr. Cajazeira performs another lancing operation on Roosevelt's leg. Rondon sits beside them, whittling a slender tree branch.

DR. CAJAZEIRA
Your fever's abated some. But you won't be able to walk much longer on this leg.

ROOSEVELT
We've reached the crest. If the gam gives out,
just give me a good shove and roll me down.

RONDON
Maybe that won't be necessary.

He holds up his handiwork--the branch stripped
and carved into a rude but acceptable CANE.

A rain begins.

EXT. ROCKY SLOPE - NIGHT

The storm drenches the river and would threa-
ten to surge away the boats, but Kermit, Lyra,
Cherrie and the others are holding onto the te-
thers for dear life, resisting the rising tide.

SERIES OF SHOTS

A gusher, the torrent fills channels, washes
mounds of earth into the river to form mud,
swells the River of Doubt.

EXT. CLIFFTOP CAMPSITE - DAY

The campers clean up after the deluge, trying to
wring out wet blankets and what few clothes
they still have left.

EXT. ROCKY SLOPE - DAY

ON KERMIT'S HAND

raw, bloody. He rips off a piece of his shorts--his
only clothing--and wraps it around his wounded
hand for a glove.

Kermit's attention is not on his hand, but upriver. Lyra stands beside him.

KERMIT
One summer in the Badlands, the Little Missouri
had a gullywasher just like that.

LYRA
Gullywasher?

They hear A RUMBLE upriver.

KERMIT
Let's move, fast!

SERIES OF SHOTS

of the men pushing and shoving with all their
strength to move the big dugouts up into the
rocks.

KERMIT
Push!

All shove with main might, get the boat lodged against a rock next to the others. Kermit hurriedly anchors it to the rock with rope as the ROAR rises in volume, finally becomes deafening, product of

THE FLOOD

not Biblical but big enough. Surging down the river is a mountain of water, driftwood, trees ripped from banks, and mud--acres of mud. The mass of debris POUNDS into the canyon, sweeping all before it, HAMMERING the canyon walls.

Kermit and the others huddle next to the boats, behind rocks.

A wall of water and mud hits, pours over them. Some are almost dislodged. They hang on desperately.

Pedrinho is swept away. He SCREAMS, trapped in a mud wall.

Kermit, clinging to a rope with his wounded hands, can only watch.

THE FLOOD WAVE

sweeps down canyon, leaving in its wake just a high tide of water--and mound of mud on the bank.

Kermit and Lyra lead the others running toward where Pedrinho disappeared. All begin to search around the mud bank, scraping back the wet earth with their hands, looking for some sign. Kermit rives mud with his knife, furiously digging here, there. Moments pass--

He comes upon a piece of cloth.

KERMIT
Here!

The others rush over, begin to claw at the mud.

MOMENTS LATER

Pedrinho is lifted out of his premature grave, gasping for air. Kermit slumps back, breathing hard.

KERMIT
I think--we all need a good bath.

SOME TIME LATER

the boats are again in the water.

Kermit takes the lead guy rope, starts to head down the river.

SERIES OF SHOTS

of Kermit and the others edging their way over rocks and thin ledges, whatever passes for a bank--feet bloodied.

EXT. CLIFFTOP - DAY

Roosevelt, Rondon and the rest of the overland expedition begin their descent with the loads.

EXT. RIVER LEDGE - DAY

Overgrown with leafy vegetation and moss.

Kermit is making his way along it, the ledge becoming narrower and narrower.

FIRE ANTS sally out, launch an attack on Kermit's hands.

Kermit grimaces, can't afford to loosen his grip and battle. They crawl over his eyes, face, bite with impunity. Kermit yells in pain and frustration.

LATER

Kermit's face is now blotched with bites. Hands and feet bloody, he trudges on ahead of the others.

Pedrinho is exhausted.

PEDRINHO
(to Lyra, meaning Kermit)
Will he never stop?

LYRA
If he stops, the paraiba will smile at us.

Pedrinho starts, looks down at the water at his
feet. The prospect of being dinner for the giant
catfish does not thrill him.

Kermit looks upward at the towering canyon
walls.

PANNING UP

the expedition at this moment is skirting the cliff
edge high above.

Roosevelt is walking with the help of Rondon's
cane. They hear a JAGUAR'S ROAR in the
jungle.

RONDON
Jaguar.

ROOSEVELT
Lordly animals, the big cats. One of the happiest
days of my life was when I bagged a lion in Africa. I sang all the way back to the camp.
(begins to sing)
"Whack falla-la, for Lanigan's Ball--"

PANNING DOWN

the song is picked up by the canyon walls. The
SOUND ECHOES down to Kermit.

He smiles, listens a moment, then begins to accompany his father.

ROOSEVELT AND KERMIT
(singing)
"Whack falla-la, for Lanigan's Ball..."

The song ECHOES up and down the walls from
father and son.

Kermit forgets some of his exhaustion and physical misery in singing the rollicking song, so
much so he doesn't realize where he's arrived.
When he does he stops, looks around.

HIS POV

he's rounded a bend and left the canyon rapids.
Ahead the river widens out into a calm smooth
cove.

POV FROM DOWNSTREAM

His WHOOP OF JOY resounds.

LATER

It's a happy group waiting on the river bank as
the overland members trudge toward them.

Roosevelt is the last to arrive. Kermit waits, re-
lieved,
happy.

LATER STILL - ON KERMIT'S LEG

as he tries to rid a BERNI FLY. Kermit cuts slits
in the skin, then squeezes out the insect. It is
not pretty. From the look of his leg, a bloody
mess, it's not the first. As he has nothing to use
as a bandage, it will have to stay that way.

EXT. RIVERBANK - DAY

A tent shelter has been erected in Roosevelt's
balsa. The rest of the boats are gathered around,
the expedition reunited.

INT. BALSA TENT - DAY

Kermit opens a flap onto this father, who's lying
there on his back, his wounded leg raised.

KERMIT
We're going to run as many rapids as we can.

ROOSEVELT
Do it, and to the devil with my comfort. Leave
me a view.

Kermit nods, opens a flap onto the river ahead.
Then gets up, starts to move toward his canoe--
but Lyra is standing in his way. He has something to say.

LYRA
I'm the healthiest man here. I'll steer his balsa.
You take the lead.

KERMIT
(a beat)
Thanks.

IN THE LEAD CANOE

Kermit steps in to the stern, the command position. Lifts paddle.

KERMIT
Let's go home.

ON RAPIDS

as Kermit's lead boat comes up to the first big
wave, then PLUNGES INTO THE CHUTE, rolling,
bouncing. The other boats follow right behind.

SERIES OF SHOTS

--The boats shuttled and rocked.
--Kermit shouting commands, directing, chur-
ning his paddle with unrelenting energy.
--In the tent, Roosevelt holding on.
--His balsa, the last of the group, rounding a
bend.

ON KERMIT'S FACE

indomitable, rushing toward FRAME, the spit-
ting image of his father when he charged up San
Juan Hill.

EXT. SMOOTH WATER - DAY

All the boats paddling a long stretch where there
is little current. The sky is clear. The sun beats
down.

KERMIT (V.O.)
On the broad river the sun hung above us all the
day like a molten ball and broiled us as if the river were a grid on which we were made fast.

ANGLE ON ROOSEVELT

in the tent, sweating profusely.

KERMIT (V.O.)
To a sick man it must have been intolerable.

IN ROOSEVELT'S TENT

great cascades of sweat pour down the invalid's red, swollen face. Dr. Cajazeira leans down to begin his incisions. The scalpel slices through the infected flesh.

EXT. ANOTHER PART OF THE RIVER - DAY

The sun is again blazing.

SUPER: APRIL 15, 1914

ANGLE ON PEDRINHO

in the prow of Kermit's canoe. He paddles as if in slow motion, his arms lead blocks from weariness. In the stern Kermit paddles with a steady rhythm, as if he's indefatigable. Pedrinho turns, eyes him with amazement.

PEDRINHO
Bwana Dandy--

ANGLE ON KERMIT

the name is absurdly out of place. He is a mess.

KERMIT
I know you're exhausted, Pedrinho. Paddle when you can.

Pedrinho looks back at the other boats.

PEDRINHO
They fall behind.

KERMIT
We'll pull them if we have to.

This prospect makes Pedrinho wilt even further.

PEDRINHO
Antonio saw a cutting on a rubber tree last
night.

KERMIT
The night before he saw his grandmother baking
a wedding cake. He's delirious.

PEDRINHO
But if he really saw it, and if the rubber gathe-
rers come up here--

A BARACA

a rubber gatherer's hut, comes into view. For a
moment Kermit and Pedrinho just stare, letting
the current take them to a fuller view of this
sight their sore eyes don't quite believe.

A BLACK MAN comes out of the baraca, watches
them arrive.

The rest of the expedition see the hut too. They erupt in CHEERS.

ROOSEVELT raises up, rips back the tent flap for a look.

The camaradas fire RIFLE SHOTS of celebration in the air.

The black man, the baraca's owner, mistakes them for a wild crew of banditos, turns and hightails it into the jungle.

EXT. AT THE BARACA - DAY

The boats are drawn up, everyone out including Roosevelt who stands with the aid of his cane.

Rondon and a couple of camaradas are leading the baraca owner out of the jungle, Rondon filling his ears with profuse explanations.

RONDON
(to the expedition)
I present to you--

MARQUES
Ramundo Jose Marques.
(proudly bowing)

RONDON
Ramundo Jose Marques, we have one question for you.
(nodding to Roosevelt)

ROOSEVELT
Where the devil are we?

Marques thinks about this a long moment, then
says very proudly:

MARQUES
Brazil!

LATER

While Rondon and Roosevelt look over a map,
other members of the expedition are conducting
intense negotiations with Ramundo Jose
Marques.

Some have already bartered for a piece of bread
or meat and are ravenously devouring. Marques
is like a vendor at a busy street market, and he
is no slouch at bargaining.

MARQUES
You catch chicken, good price. Duck not for sale.

Some camaradas shout protest at this depriva-
tion.

MARQUES
Duck like my brother!

A wad of MONEY is shoved in his face. Marques
grabs it.

MARQUES
(shrugs)
Take brother.

Pedrinho has taken Marques at his word and is
running around the yard after a SQUAWKING
CHICKEN. He is having little success corralling
it.

Cherrie comes away from his dealing with a can
of condensed milk. Kermit is sitting on the
doorstep of the baraca.

CHERRIE
Would you take a look at that.

He holds up the can as if it were treasure.

CHERRIE
At this moment in time, nothing in the world
could taste better.

Kermit counters with his own trade, a BOTTLE
OF VERMOUTH.

THE CAN OF CONDENSED MILK

is let fall PLOP in the dust.

A SHORT TIME LATER - CHERRIE AND KERMIT

are getting royally drunk. They down drinks,
pour another.

A FLY lands in Kermit's glass. He picks it out, stows it in the ragged pocket of his shorts.

KERMIT
Just in case.

They laugh, drunk and punch drunk at the same time.
 Lyra comes over to Kermit who gives him a long look, then throws him the bottle.

KERMIT
Finish it.

Lyra cradles the bottle, rubs it like a precious gem, then polishes it off in one glorious gulp. Cherrie and Kermit applaud.

PEDRINHO

is slumped, exhausted. The chicken cavorts with impunity.

PEDRINHO
I pay. You catch.

MARQUES
Fucking river too much fuck you.

EXT. RIVERBANK - DAY

The boats head away newly provisioned.
Marques the rubber gatherer goes with them. He

is chattering away in Portuguese and seems a very happy man. Kermit, in the lead canoe but momentarily side by side with his father's balsa, translates for his benefit.

KERMIT
He says, rubber trade fucked, no fucking market, him fucked too, but thanks to us, Ramundo Jose Marques no more give fuck.

ROOSEVELT
Eloquent fellow.

SERIES OF SHOTS - ON THE RIVER

Marques acts as guide, pointing out the best channels for the canoes.

Rondon holds a map spread out on his lap, is drawing a line tracing the route of the River of Doubt--debouching into the Madeira, which then flows into the Amazon.

ROOSEVELT (V.O.)
It was extraordinary to realize we had put on the map a river 1000 miles long, about the size of the Rhine or Elbe, and no geographer had any idea of its existence.

They slide easily through a stretch of rapids.

Cherrie is also writing in his journal.

CHERRIE
There were still two long weeks of travel with many rapids ahead of us but from that day on the Rio Roosevelt was no longer a River of Doubt to us.

EXT. HAMLET PORT - DAY

The expedition members, clad now in clean new clothes, board a river steamer.

Rondon tarries with Roosevelt and Kermit and Lyra, regarding the canoes which are tied to the dock.

RONDON
Battered and chipped, like us.

ROOSEVELT
They're like faithless lovers. They gave no end of trouble and you're happy to be rid of the headaches and misery, but you miss them.

EXT. MANAUS - DAY

ESTABLISHING SHOT of the city--

ROOSEVELT (V.O.)
At Manaus we found Miller, and glad indeed we were to see him.

SHOT. The members of the respective expeditions mingle.

ROOSEVELT (V.O.)
His expedition had been successful, though not
without a loss of canoes, their scientific instru-
ments and most of their notes.

EXT. MANAUS HARBOR - DAY

A cargo boat waits at the dock in b.g. The camaradas are all lined up. Roosevelt is going along
the line, plunking gold sovereigns in the palm of
each man, after which he vigorously shakes
their hand. Trailing behind him, Kermit seconds
the handshakes.

ROOSEVELT
Gold sovereigns. Don't spend them all in the fleshpots of Manaus!

Kermit translates this for their benefit.

ANTONIO
We've made a vow. Each of us is going to keep
one as a souvenir. Of our trip with you.

ROOSEVELT
And the rest?

Antonio answers in Portuguese. Kermit translates.

KERMIT
The fleshpots.

A SMALL PODIUM

has been set up for the press, many of whom are
American, the same reporters seen at the outset.
They watch in amazement as Roosevelt, walking
with the aid of a new store-bought cane, makes
his way to the podium with Rondon.

Roosevelt waves his cane energetically.

ROOSEVELT
Hello boys! You see I still have my big stick.

YOUNG REPORTER
My God. He must have lost 35 pounds.

MOMENTS LATER - INTERCUT PRESS CONFE-
RENCE AND ACTION NEARBY

RONDON
We have had a hard and somewhat dangerous
but very successful trip.

CHERRIE

is on the gangplank of the cargo boat, supervising the unloading of what animal specimens he
has managed to save.

ROOSEVELT
I was a pretty sick man, but I'm better now.

The young reporter is interviewing Dr. Cajazeira
separately, taking copious notes.

YOUNG REPORTER
(reacting to what he's hearing)
My God!

RONDON
I've made many explorations into the Amazon. I
expect to make many more. This one I know I
will never forget.

Lyra fingers Kermit's new suit--it's elegant, expensive but-

LYRA
Cotton!

KERMIT
Manaus has a shortage of silk.

ROOSEVELT
Each of us North Americans is longing for the
homely things so dear to him, for the home
people--and for the one dearest of all.

LYRA
(to Kermit)
You should be up there.

KERMIT
That's not what matters.

He shakes hands with Lyra. Then after a beat,
they hug like brothers.

LATER

prior to walking up the plank to depart, Roosevelt, Kermit and Cherrie pause for final handshakes and farewells to the Brazilians.

RONDON
I pray we will meet again.

ROOSEVELT
We're proud to have been your companions.

LATER

the cargo boat pulls out with a HORN WHISTLE,
shouts and waves from shore to deck.

INTERCUT BOAT AND SHORE

as all the survivors of the River of Doubt make
their farewells, Rondon and Lyra and Dr. Cajazeira are joined by the camaradas in yelling fond
good-byes, the Americans on the boat respon-
ding heartily in kind.

When the boat's turgid wake stretches far out to
sea,the press begin to disperse, all but the
young reporter who has collared Rondon.

YOUNG REPORTER
Colonel Rondon, what really happened on that
river?

Rondon reflects a long moment.

RONDON
We learned humility.

INT. ROOSEVELT'S CABIN - NIGHT

ROOSEVELT'S VISION - SERIES OF SHOTS

It's the jungle of the River of Doubt, only more
horrifying. Vines creep, ants the size of lions
stampede toward FRAME, IMMENSE SERPENTS
COIL, and somewhere a WOMAN WEEPS. A
ghastly nightmare, only the dreamer isn't asleep
and dreaming.

Roosevelt lies wide awake in his bunk, shivering
from an attack of fever, watching the horrors
that seem to be unfolding on the wall opposite.

HIS IMAGINED POV

The SERPENTS COIL around the woman--Alice.
She cries out for « Theodore! Theodore." Sweat
and tears pour down Roosevelt's face.

EXT. SHIP DECK - DAY

Roosevelt reclines in a lounge chair, blanket
around legs and waist. A knee-high stack of

books to be devoured rests on one side; Kermit
kneels on the other.

A group of YOUNG CHILDREN run up, led by a
little BLONDE GIRL. There is also a small dark-
haired boy, JIMMY, clutching a teddy bear.

BLONDE GIRL
Colonel Roosevelt, are you going to tell us another ghost story tonight?

ROOSEVELT
Why of course I am. This one takes place in the
deepest darkest jungle.

Excited squeals all around.

ROOSEVELT
Eight o'clock sharp, all hands on deck.

More excited squeals, the children scurrying off-
-all but Jimmy who clutches his bear.

ROOSEVELT
Yes Jimmy, you can bring your-
(forcing the word out)
teddy bear.

Jimmy grins, runs off after the others.

ROOSEVELT
I detest that nickname.

Roosevelt reaches down for a stack of books, leans back in his chair. The cost of the effort shows on his face.

KERMIT
How was your night?

Roosevelt shakes his head at the memory.

ROOSEVELT
Like the others. That river put a poison in my blood. It will plague me the rest of my life.

Kermit pulls up the blanket for him. Roosevelt reflects.

ROOSEVELT
But we did something in that jungle. It didn't beat us. We made it. By George, we made it.

He looks pensive for a moment, then:

ROOSEVELT
Son, I'd appreciate it if you'd help me to my cabin.

He holds out his hand. Kermit takes it, helps him up.

EXT. ENGLISH CHURCH - MADRID - DAY

Kermit and Belle Willard stand in resplendent wedding garb before the minister. Roosevelt stands nearby, best man.

INT. AMERICAN EMBASSY - DAY

The reception.

SERIES OF SHOTS of wedding guests, a joyous
Kermit and Belle, a gigantic cake, limitless
champagne, a mountain of gifts for bride and
groom.

A dance is in progress, the VIRGINIA REEL.
Conspicuous among the dancers is Roosevelt.
Showing no traces of illness, he highsteps it with
his oldtime élan with his wife Edith.

Once or twice they bump into the newlyweds,
who dance with grace and style.

The dance ends to the applause of all.

MOMENTS LATER

Roosevelt and Edith, cradling glasses of punch,
are with Kermit and Belle, eyeing the immense
array of wedding gifts.

ROOSEVELT
You'll need a Conestoga wagon to haul all this
back to the States.

They stop and stare at an incongruous sight
among the gaudy presents: a dozen plain woo-
den barrels.

BELLE
What's that?

KERMIT
Cherrie's wedding gift. 30 gallons of his maple
syrup.

ROOSEVELT
(to Belle)
I hope you like flapjacks.

A WESTERN UNION MESSENGER enters the
room, a package under his arm.

The messenger comes up with the package, gives
it to Kermit. who eyes the return address.

KERMIT
Special delivery--from Brazil!

Roosevelt, Belle, Edith and some other guests
crowd around. Kermit takes out a card, gives the
package to Belle to open. He reads quickly.
Smiles shyly, hands the card to his father who
reads aloud
for the others--

ROOSEVELT
"Dear Bwana Dandy. Your eminent father is fond
of saying, 'In the wilderness a man reveals himself as he truly is.' Please accept this small gift
from your grateful companions on the River of
Doubt, Colonel Candido Rondon, Lt. Joao Lyra,
Dr. Cajazeira and all the camaradas."

Belle holds up the contents of the package--a sort of PARCHMENT SCROLL.

Kermit takes the SCROLL, unrolls it, regards it for a moment. When he speaks there is a catch in his voice.

KERMIT
God bless all of them.

Roosevelt puts his arm around Kermit's neck, hugs him affectionately.

INSERT - THE SCROLL

is an updated MAP OF WESTERN BRAZIL. Conspicuous in the Amazon Basin is a large state called "RONDONIA."

MOVING CLOSER to the multitude of rivers marking like arteries the heart of Rondonia, we note the "RIO ROOSEVELT."

MOVING STILL CLOSER to the map, we see an affluent stream entering the Rio Roosevelt: it is now called "RIO KERMIT."

FADE OUT:

THE END

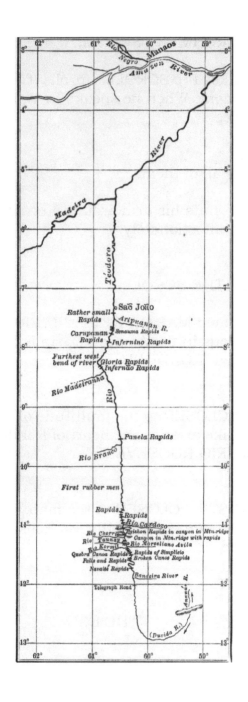

Martin Copeland is a screenwriter, playwright and author of the novels THE BOYS FROM DOG-TOWN, LA LOVE STORIES and MANHUNT IN FRANCE.

Made in United States
Troutdale, OR
08/18/2024

22095200R00141